New Directions for
Higher Education

Martin Kramer
EDITOR-IN-CHIEF

The Challenge of Balancing Faculty Careers and Family Work

John W. Curtis
EDITOR

Number 130 • Summer 2005
Jossey-Bass
San Francisco

THE CHALLENGE OF BALANCING FACULTY CAREERS AND FAMILY WORK
John W. Curtis (ed.)
New Directions for Higher Education, no. 130
Martin Kramer, Editor-in-Chief

Microfilm copies of issues and articles are available in 16mm and 35mm, as well as microfiche in 105mm, through University Microfilms Inc., 300 North Zeeb Road, Ann Arbor, Michigan 48106-1346.

NEW DIRECTIONS FOR HIGHER EDUCATION (ISSN 0271-0560, electronic ISSN 1536-0741) is part of The Jossey-Bass Higher and Adult Education Series and is published quarterly by Wiley Subscription Services, Inc., a Wiley company, at Jossey-Bass, 989 Market Street, San Francisco, California 94103-1741. Periodicals Postage Paid at San Francisco, California, and at additional mailing offices. POSTMASTER: Send address changes to New Directions for Higher Education, Jossey-Bass, 989 Market Street, San Francisco, California 94103-1741.

New Directions for Higher Education is indexed in Current Index to Journals in Education (ERIC); Higher Education Abstracts.

SUBSCRIPTIONS cost $80 for individuals and $170 for institutions, agencies, and libraries. See ordering information page at end of journal.

EDITORIAL CORRESPONDENCE should be sent to the Editor-in-Chief, Martin Kramer, 2807 Shasta Road, Berkeley, California 94708-2011.

Cover photograph © Digital Vision

www.josseybass.com

Contents

EDITOR'S NOTES

The "challenge" referred to in the title of this volume, that of balancing faculty careers with family responsibilities, has been recognized in the higher education literature for at least a decade (Friedman, Rimsky, and Johnson, 1996). But even before it became a topic for research and policy formulation, the challenge existed—and it was played out primarily in the lives of women academics. For decades, women who pursued advanced degrees and careers in the academy faced a series of obstacles and conflicts. The obstacles consisted of policies both written and unwritten, expectations spoken or unspoken, and discrimination both subtle and blatant. Today the legal, formal, and visible hurdles have been largely, though not entirely, removed, leaving in their stead more subtle structural disadvantages: forms of bias and discrimination that could almost be characterized as unconscious or unintended.

The conflicts women faced were those that arise when an individual's multiple roles prescribe different types of behavior. At certain points in time—likely several different points in a lifetime—the role of daughter, wife, or mother would come into conflict with the role of scholar, scientist, or professor. To this day, the resolution of such conflicts often is portrayed as a "choice" that women make. Faced with such a "choice" between fulfilling the obligations of a family role and pursuing an academic career, women have often sacrificed their careers by accepting part-time or restricted positions or by taking positions at teaching-oriented colleges that offered a more predictable workload.

This "solution" to the challenge of balancing competing roles produced inequitable outcomes because it was a constraint that imposed fewer expectations on men. Men were able to fulfill their traditional role as "breadwinner" by pursuing an academic career without constraints. Even in situations where men might want to be more involved in family responsibilities, they were likely to be encouraged to fulfill their "proper" role as full-time income earner, even when that meant a career sacrifice on the part of a wife or partner. As Mason and Goulden (2002, 2004) have pointed out, the inequities in the academic situation were actually twofold: women suffered career disadvantages, and "successful" women were also more likely to experience limitations on their ability to have as many children as they wanted.

The situation described to this point is not really one of balance at all. When faculty careers and family responsibilities have come in conflict, the academic career has prevailed. Individuals have adapted to the demands of the career rather than the other way around. This has produced inequities between men and women in academic career outcomes, in discouraging women from pursuing academic careers, and in limiting the ability of women to have their desired number of children. To the extent these inequities still clearly exist, as described in Mason and Goulden's work as well as by Laura Perna and Valerie Martin Conley in Chapters One and Two, respectively, in this volume, we can speak of continuing challenges. This includes the very subtle inequities of stereotyping and cumulative disadvantage described in Chapter Six in this volume by Joan Williams and elsewhere by Virginia Valian (1998).

However, Carol Hollenshead and her colleagues in Chapter Three, Kelly Ward and Lisa Wolf-Wendel in Chapter Four, and Saranna Thornton in Chapter Five describe many colleges and universities that have adopted policies designed to help faculty balance successful academic careers with fulfilling family lives. Many of these policies follow the recommendations of the American Association of University Professors in its "Statement of Principles on Family Responsibilities and Academic Work" (2001). To the extent that such policies redress the current imbalance between faculty careers and family, they might be seen as answering the challenge we have described. But as Ward and Wolf-Wendel and Thornton describe in this volume, there are still many obstacles to overcome before implementation of such policies can be considered successful.

Perhaps the most daunting new challenge is that of stimulating a cultural change in the academy, so that faculty members who want to make use of policies for balancing work and family feel confident in doing so. As Ward and Wolf-Wendel argue elsewhere (2004), many faculty members fear that making use of family-friendly policies will lead to negative career consequences. They fear that they will be seen as "lacking commitment" to their academic careers if they try to carve out time for their families. Drago and Colbeck (2003) have described what they refer to as "bias avoidance behavior" among faculty. This consists of various actions that faculty members take to resolve the conflict between work and family by either avoiding family obligations in the first place or disguising the amount of time spent in family caregiving. Such a situation cannot produce a satisfactory balance in the lives of faculty.

Thus, the challenge of the title remains. And answering that challenge requires a fundamental recasting of the problem itself. As long as the conflict between family responsibilities and faculty careers is viewed as an individual problem, the solutions will continue to constitute a structural disadvantage for women. For men, the imbalance has been different. Increasingly, men want to devote more time to child care and other family responsibilities. As Joan Williams points out in Chapter Six, although they have not experienced the same structural disadvantage in terms of career, men have also been constrained in their ability to balance work and family. They too perceive a conflict with an academic career that demands a full-time, overtime, and lifetime commitment.

The premise of this volume is that the challenge of balancing faculty careers and family work is not one that individuals—men or women—should face alone. It is also a challenge for colleges and universities if they are to recruit and retain the most able faculty. As long as women are at a structural disadvantage in pursuing faculty careers to the full extent of their abilities, colleges and universities are not drawing from the complete pool of potential faculty members. And if academic careers are not seen as sufficiently attractive, both men and women of ability will choose other employment.

Beyond even the imperative for higher education institutions to employ the best faculty, there is a broader consideration for the future of higher education. Women have faced barriers to academic advancement in part because of the conflict between work and family. As documented in Chapters One and Two, in many cases this has led women to "choose" employment in contingent academic positions: part-time teaching, usually on a course-by-course basis, or limited-term full-time non-tenure-track positions. These positions are contingent in the sense that they are designated at the outset as short term, so that continued employment is usually contingent on being rehired after a single term or academic year. Part-time positions generally do not involve extensive searches, and the hiring decisions are usually in the hands of a single administrator. Outside a unionized setting, part-time faculty generally do not have access to full protections of academic due process with regard to hiring and (non)reappointment actions. Full-time term faculty may be selected on the basis of a more traditional search process and may have responsibilities similar to those of tenure-track faculty members. But they also may not have recourse to full academic due process in the case of a dismissal or lack of reappointment, and their positions certainly do not hold the long-term career prospects of tenure-track positions.

The increasing use of contingent faculty positions to meet growing enrollments is part of a broader transformation of colleges and universities toward a more corporate model. Faculty are increasingly viewed as solely a cost factor and weighed against "bottom-line" calculations—even though the vast majority of higher education institutions are still categorized as nonprofit organizations operating for the common good.

To the extent that women are overrepresented in contingent positions, their academic freedom has been compromised. As part-time teachers, they are not fully free to introduce controversial subjects or challenging assignments into the classroom, for fear that a single complaint could mean the loss of their position. In visiting or other term faculty appointments, they do not have the support and job security necessary to pursue a scholarly agenda over the course of several years. This is more than just an individual cost. It is a cost to institutions and to higher education and society as a whole. Our higher education system is based on the free exchange of ideas in both teaching and scholarship, and a structural constraint on the academic freedom of one entire category represents a loss for the system as a whole.

Women continue to face barriers in entering and advancing in academic careers. Men too experience the tension between dedication to career and a desire to play an active role in their families. In the context of the rise of contingent appointments as the modal situation for new faculty hires and a growing emphasis on corporate models for higher education, both institutions and faculty need to consider how to maintain a faculty fully engaged in teaching, research, and institutional governance with academic freedom protected by tenure, while at the same time making room for new voices and new perspectives in the academic community. Workable measures to enable faculty to balance their academic careers with their lives off-campus are one way of meeting that challenge. Our hope is that this volume can make a contribution toward developing a more workable balance.

John W. Curtis
Editor

References

American Association of University Professors. "Statement of Principles on Family Responsibilities and Academic Work." 2001. http://www.aaup.org/statements/REPORTS/re01fam.htm.

Drago, R., and Colbeck, C. "The Mapping Project: Exploring the Terrain of U.S. Colleges and Universities for Faculty and Families: Final Report for the Alfred P. Sloan Foundation." University Park: Pennsylvania State University, 2003. http://lsir.la.psu.edu/workfam/mappingproject.htm.

Friedman, D. E., Rimsky, C., and Johnson, A. A. *College and University Reference Guide to Work/Family Programs.* New York: Families and Work Institute, 1996.

Mason, M. A., and Goulden, M. "Do Babies Matter?" *Academe,* 2002, 88(6), 21–27.

Mason, M. A., and Goulden, M. "Do Babies Matter (Part II)? Closing the Baby Gap." *Academe,* 2004, 90(6), 10–15.

Valian, V. *Why So Slow? The Advancement of Women.* Cambridge, Mass.: MIT Press, 1998.

Ward, K., and Wolf-Wendel, L. "Fear Factor: How Safe Is It to Make Time for Family?" *Academe,* 2004, 90(6), 28–31.

JOHN W. CURTIS is director of research for the American Association of University Professors in Washington, D.C.

1

Institutional leaders should consider the consequences of policies, practices, and social forces that force women to choose between work and family.

The Relationship Between Family and Employment Outcomes

Laura Perna

The representation of women among the nation's college and university faculty has been increasing since the 1960s (U.S. Department of Education, 2003). Despite this progress, gender inequities remain in various aspects of faculty life, including such employment outcomes as salaries, academic rank, and tenure status, as well as in such family outcomes as marriage and children. While certainly not all women and men desire marriage or children, or both, persistent differences in the shares of women and men faculty who are married or have children, or both, suggest that the nature of faculty employment has disparate impacts on the family decisions and lives of women and men faculty.

The magnitude of the difficulties that are associated with managing work and family demands is demonstrated at least in part by the frequency of related discussions in trade publications that are targeted to college and university faculty and administrators. A few recent titles from the *Chronicle of Higher Education* indicate the nature of the concerns: "How Babies Alter Careers: Having Children Often Bumps Women off the Tenure Track, a New Study Shows" (Wilson, 2003), "Singing the Babies Blues: If Having Children on the Tenure Track Is a Career Killer, Is Having Them in Graduate School Any Better?" (Williams, 2004), and "Job Sharing on the Tenure Track: To Make Time for Their Children, Two Academics Opt to Share a Faculty Position and a Half" (Rubley, 2004). In December 2003 the *Chronicle of Higher Education* hosted a live one-hour colloquy entitled, "Babies, Mothers, and Academic Careers," during which Mary Ann Mason, dean of the Graduate Division at the University of California, Berkeley, electronically received and responded to comments and questions. The

NEW DIRECTIONS FOR HIGHER EDUCATION, no. 130, Summer 2005   © Wiley Periodicals, Inc.

Association of American Colleges and Universities devoted its winter 2004 issue of the electronic publication *On Campus with Women* to the work/family balancing act of college and university faculty and students.

This chapter describes what is known from research about the relationship between work and family among college and university faculty in the United States. Descriptive analyses of data from the 1999 National Study of Postsecondary Faculty (NSOPF:99), a cross-sectional survey sponsored by the U.S. Department of Education, National Center for Education Statistics, supplement the literature review. The descriptive analyses examine selected work and family characteristics of women and men faculty, where faculty are defined as individuals working at nonproprietary two-year and four-year institutions with faculty status and at least some for-credit instructional responsibilities. The data are weighted so that they are representative of the population of faculty nationwide in fall 1998. The chapter also describes two frameworks for understanding the relationship between family and employment outcomes and identifies the barriers to achieving gender equity in family and employment. The chapter concludes by offering recommendations for institutional policy and practices.

Sex Differences in the Employment Outcomes of College and University Faculty

Women represented 41 percent of teaching faculty with the rank of instructor or higher at colleges and universities nationwide in 1999–2000, up from 23 percent in 1969–1970 (U.S. Department of Education, 2003). Nonetheless, although women now represent a higher share of the nation's faculty, the magnitude of progress varies by institutional type, academic field, and employment status. For example, in fall 1998, women represented a higher share of full-time faculty employed at public two-year colleges (50 percent) than at public (30 percent) and private (26 percent) research universities. The representation of women among full-time faculty in fall 1998 also varied by academic discipline, ranging from 9 percent in engineering and 14 percent in physical sciences to 64 percent in teacher education and 96 percent in nursing (U.S. Department of Education, 2003).

In terms of employment status, women are relatively concentrated in less prestigious, and more tenuous, positions. About half (48 percent) of women faculty, but only one-third (38 percent) of men faculty, were employed part time rather than full time in fall 1999 (U.S. Department of Education, 2003). A higher share of women than men faculty held non-tenure-track positions (24 percent versus 15 percent) in fall 1998 (Bradburn and Sikora, 2002). Only 40 percent of women full-time faculty, but 60 percent of men full-time faculty, held tenured positions in both fall 1992 and fall 1998, illustrating not only the magnitude but also the persistence of the gender gap in tenured positions (Parsad and Glover, 2002). In fall 1999, women represented only 21 percent of faculty with the highest rank of full professor but 45 percent of assistant professors, 51 percent of instructors, and 54 percent of lecturers (U.S. Department of Education, 2003).

Sex Differences in the Family Outcomes of College and University Faculty

Women faculty also differ from men faculty in terms of family outcomes. Descriptive analyses of data from the NSOPF:99 show that smaller shares of women than men are married, and higher shares of women than men are separated, divorced, or widowed regardless of employment status, institutional type, tenure status, or academic rank. In fall 1998, 74 percent of all men faculty were married, compared with only 65 percent of all women faculty. About 16 percent of all women, but only 9 percent of all men, were separated, divorced, or widowed. Table 1.1 shows that the gap in the percentages of women and men faculty who were married was smaller among those employed part time (11 percentage points) than among those employed full time (17 percentage points). Among both full-time and part-time faculty, the percentage who were separated, divorced, or widowed was about twice as high among women as among men. Table 1.1 shows that 15 percent of women full-time faculty were separated, widowed, or divorced in fall 1998, compared with only 8 percent of men full-time faculty.

Among full-time faculty, sex differences in the percentages who were married were largest at public doctoral and private four-year institutions (21 percentage points) and smallest at public two-year institutions (6 percentage points). Table 1.1 shows that 83 percent of men, but 62 percent of women, full-time faculty at public doctoral institutions were married. At public two-year institutions, 76 percent of men full-time faculty were married compared with 71 percent of women full-time faculty. The proportion of faculty who were separated, divorced, or widowed was twice as high among women as among men at public doctoral institutions, private doctoral institutions, public four-year colleges, and private four-year colleges.

Sex differences in marital status are also larger among faculty with the highest-status positions: tenured and full professor. Table 1.1 shows that in fall 1998, 83 percent of men full-time tenured faculty, but only 63 percent of women full-time tenured faculty, were married, a 20 percentage point gap. About 86 percent of male full-time full professors, but only 63 percent of female full-time full professors, were married (a 23 percentage point gap). Sex differences in the share of full-time faculty who were married were smaller among faculty in the less prestigious positions, namely non-tenure-track faculty (10 percentage points), faculty at institutions without a tenure system (11 percentage points), and instructors (4 percentage points). The proportion of faculty who were separated, divorced, or widowed was about twice as high among women as among men at all tenure statuses and academic ranks except instructor.

Table 1.1. Distribution of Women and Men Full-Time Faculty by Marital Status and Institutional Type, Tenure Status, and Academic Rank, Fall 1998

			Marital Status			
Characteristic	Sex	Total	Single, Never Married	Married	Living with Someone	Separated, Divorced, Widowed
Total	Total	100.0	12.3	73.6	2.5	11.6
	Men	100.0	10.1	79.4	2.0	8.5
	Women	100.0	15.7	65.0	3.2	16.1
Employment status						
Full-time	Men	100.0	9.0	80.5	2.3	8.2
	Women	100.0	16.9	63.6	4.3	15.3
Part-time	Men	100.0	12.1	77.2	1.7	9.0
	Women	100.0	14.3	66.7	1.9	17.1
Institutional type[a]						
Public doctoral	Men	100.0	8.0	82.5	2.7	6.9
	Women	100.0	18.7	61.8	4.8	14.7
Public four-year	Men	100.0	10.4	77.7	2.6	9.4
	Women	100.0	17.7	57.7	4.9	19.6
Private doctoral	Men	100.0	9.9	82.3	2.1	5.7
	Women	100.0	14.5	68.0	6.0	11.6
Private four-year	Men	100.0	9.9	81.4	1.3	7.3
	Women	100.0	20.2	60.9	5.0	13.9
Public two-year	Men	100.0	8.3	75.9	2.1	13.6
	Women	100.0	12.0	70.5	2.1	15.4
Tenure status[a]						
Tenured	Men	100.0	5.9	83.2	2.2	8.7
	Women	100.0	16.0	62.6	4.0	17.4
On tenure track	Men	100.0	14.5	74.7	2.1	8.7
	Women	100.0	19.0	59.9	5.2	15.9
Not on tenure track	Men	100.0	15.0	75.1	3.1	6.7
	Women	100.0	17.2	65.2	5.4	12.2
No tenure system	Men	100.0	10.0	81.8	1.7	6.5
	Women	100.0	15.6	70.8	1.5	12.0
Academic rank[a]						
Full professor	Men	100.0	4.6	85.9	1.5	8.0
	Women	100.0	16.2	62.8	4.4	16.6
Associate	Men	100.0	7.4	82.1	2.9	7.6
	Women	100.0	16.6	63.2	4.1	16.1
Assistant	Men	100.0	16.3	73.5	2.9	7.3
	Women	100.0	19.8	59.6	5.6	15.1
Instructor	Men	100.0	12.1	73.4	2.0	12.5
	Women	100.0	14.4	69.8	1.7	14.1

Note: The sample is limited to individuals with faculty status and at least some for-credit instructional duties.

[a]The sample is further limited to individuals employed full time.

Source: Analyses of NSOPF:99. Data weighted by WEIGHT.

A smaller percentage of women than men full-time faculty have at least one dependent (the best available measure of parental status), regardless of employment status, institutional type, tenure status, and academic rank. Table 1.2 shows that in fall 1998, 69 percent of men, but only 51 percent of women, had at least one dependent, a difference of 18 percentage points. Sex differences in these rates did not vary based on employment status. Among full-time faculty, the gap between the percentages of women and men who had at least one dependent was comparable in magnitude (20 percentage points) at public doctoral, private doctoral, and public four-year institutions and somewhat smaller (16 percentage points) at private four-year and public two-year institutions. Observed sex differences in the percentage of full-time faculty with at least one dependent were smaller among faculty in non-tenure-track positions (16 percentage points) than among faculty who were tenured (22 percentage points) and faculty who worked at an institution with no tenure system (22 percentage points). The sex gap in the shares of full-time faculty with at least one dependent was also smaller among instructors (9 percentage points) than among full professors (22 percentage points), associate professors (25 percentage points), and assistant professors (18 percentage points).

The Relationship Between Family and Employment Outcomes

Descriptive analyses show the relative overrepresentation of women among part-time rather than full-time faculty, faculty at public two-year rather than research universities, non-tenure-track faculty rather than tenured faculty, and assistant professors and instructors rather than full professors. Descriptive analyses also show lower rates of being married and having children for women than for men at all types of institutions and in all types of positions, but they also suggest that the gender gaps in marital and parental status are smaller among faculty at less prestigious institutions (such as public two-year colleges) and in less prestigious positions (for example, instructors) than among other faculty. Nonetheless, descriptive analyses do not reveal the extent to which sex differences in family outcomes are related to sex differences in employment outcomes after taking into account alternative explanations for the observed relationships. This section summarizes what is known from research about the relationship between family and employment outcomes.

Researchers have examined the extent to which, after controlling for other variables, marital and parental status are related to a variety of employment outcomes among college and university faculty, including employment status (Ferber and Hoffman, 1997; Perna, 2001; Wolfinger, Mason, and Goulden, 2004), tenure and promotion (Bellas, 1992; Mason and Goulden, 2004; Perna, 2005; Wolfinger, Mason, and Goulden, 2004), and salaries (Barbezat, 1988; Bellas, 1992; Toutkoushian, 1998). Researchers (Bellas and

**Table 1.2. Distribution of Women and Men Full-Time Faculty
by Parental Status and Institutional Type, Tenure Status,
and Academic Rank, Fall 1998**

| Characteristic | Sex | Total | Number of Dependents | | | |
			None	1	2	3 or More
Total	Total	100.0	38.7	22.8	19.7	18.8
	Men	100.0	31.5	24.3	20.5	23.7
	Women	100.0	49.4	20.5	18.6	11.5
Employment status						
Full time	Men	100.0	30.1	24.5	20.7	24.6
	Women	100.0	48.8	21.2	19.4	10.6
Part time	Men	100.0	34.0	23.9	20.2	21.9
	Women	100.0	50.0	19.7	17.6	12.7
Institutional type[a]						
Public doctoral	Men	100.0	29.9	22.9	22.3	24.9
	Women	100.0	51.1	19.4	19.0	10.5
Private doctoral	Men	100.0	25.2	22.9	23.8	28.0
	Women	100.0	45.7	20.5	22.1	11.6
Public four-year	Men	100.0	34.0	25.2	17.6	23.1
	Women	100.0	54.2	22.0	15.7	8.1
Private four-year	Men	100.0	31.8	26.0	17.6	24.6
	Women	100.0	48.2	20.7	20.0	11.2
Public two-year	Men	100.0	28.3	27.8	21.4	22.5
	Women	100.0	43.9	23.3	21.3	11.6
Tenure status[a]						
Tenured	Men	100.0	28.8	26.7	21.4	23.2
	Women	100.0	50.7	21.7	17.3	10.3
On tenure track	Men	100.0	32.6	18.9	20.0	28.5
	Women	100.0	50.4	22.1	18.9	8.7
Not on tenure track	Men	100.0	35.4	19.6	20.1	24.8
	Women	100.0	47.0	20.4	19.9	12.6
No tenure system	Men	100.0	26.5	28.6	18.2	26.8
	Women	100.0	42.8	19.5	26.3	11.4
Academic rank[a]						
Full professor	Men	100.0	30.0	28.8	20.2	21.0
	Women	100.0	52.2	22.6	16.7	8.5
Associate	Men	100.0	24.7	22.7	22.5	30.1
	Women	100.0	49.7	21.1	18.7	10.5
Assistant	Men	100.0	33.5	19.1	20.9	26.6
	Women	100.0	51.4	19.4	20.1	9.1
Instructor	Men	100.0	32.6	24.2	20.1	23.1
	Women	100.0	42.4	23.6	21.5	12.5

Note: The sample is limited to individuals with faculty status and at least some for-credit instructional duties.

[a]The sample is further limited to individuals employed full time.

Source: Analyses of NSOPF:99. Data weighted by WEIGHT.

Toutkoushian, 1999; Creamer, 1998) have also examined the relationship between family status and research productivity, a primary determinant of such outcomes as tenure, rank, and salaries.

With a few exceptions (for example, the examination of tenure and promotion by Wolfinger, Mason, and Goulden, 2004), research generally shows that the relationship between family and employment outcomes is different for women than for men. Most research suggests that men faculty benefit from being married in terms of such outcomes as employment status, tenure status, salaries, and productivity (Bellas, 1992; Mason and Goulden, 2004; Perna, 2001; Toutkoushian, 1998).

For example, after controlling for education, experience, and publications, Ferber and Hoffman (1997) found that neither the probability of being employed at a research or doctoral university nor the probability of holding the highest rank of full professor was related to such measures of family responsibilities as geographical distance from the current partner, level of education of partners, number of years partners were employed at the same institution, number of children, and number of years children spent in the household, for women or men faculty employed at two-year and four-year colleges and universities in the state of Illinois in 1993. For men, the number of years spent with partners was associated with a lower likelihood of working at a research or doctoral university, but a higher likelihood of holding the rank of full professor. The number of years spent with partners may be a proxy for geographical mobility in the former relationship and a proxy for household support in the latter (Ferber and Hoffman, 1997).

Wolfinger, Mason, and Goulden (2004) used data from the 1978 to 1994 Survey of Doctorate Recipients to examine the effects of family formation on three outcomes: holding a tenure-track faculty position, being promoted from assistant to tenured associate professor, and being promoted from associate to full professor. Their analyses show that after controlling for time to the doctoral degree, year of the doctorate, field of study, prestige of the doctoral program and employing institution, race, and age, women with children under age six and married women were less likely than women without children and single women, respectively, to hold tenure-track positions. Marital status and having a child under age six were unrelated to both promotion to tenured associate professor and promotion to full professor among women and men (Wolfinger, Mason, and Goulden, 2004).

In an examination of the relationship between family responsibilities and employment status, Perna (2001) used data from the NSOPF:93 to focus on the experiences of junior faculty: individuals with faculty status who held tenure-track and non-tenure-track positions rather than tenured positions in fall 1992. After controlling for educational attainment, experience, academic field, and institutional characteristics, the probability of holding a non-tenure-track position was related to marital and parental status, but the relationship was different for women than for men. Specifically, men with at least one child were less likely to hold a (lower-status) full-time, non-tenure-track position than they were to hold a (higher-status) full-time, tenure-track position, even after controlling for differences in other variables. In contrast, women who were married were more likely to hold a (lower-status) part-time, non-tenure-track position than a (higher-status) full-time tenure-track position after controlling for other variables (Perna, 2001).

In contrast to Wolfinger, Mason, and Goulden (2004), Perna (2005) found, using data from the NSOPF:99, that the relationship between family and two employment outcomes, tenure and rank, varied by sex. Among full-time faculty working at four-year colleges and universities in fall 1998, having dependents and having a spouse or partner who was employed at the same institution were both unrelated to tenure and rank among women faculty after controlling for differences in education, experience, productivity, academic field, and institutional characteristics. In contrast, men appeared to benefit in terms of their tenure status and rank from having dependents and in terms of their rank from being married. Compared to men with four or more dependents, men without dependents were more likely to hold non-tenure-track than tenured positions and were more likely to hold the lowest academic ranks of instructor and lecturer than the highest rank of full professor. Men with a spouse or partner who was employed at the same institution were less likely than men who never married to hold the ranks of assistant professor, instructor, and lecturer than the rank of full professor. Moreover, men with a spouse or partner who was not employed in higher education (and perhaps not employed at all) were less likely than men who never married to hold the ranks of associate or assistant professor than the rank of full professor (Perna, 2005).

Using data from the National Science Foundation's Survey of Doctorate Recipients, Mason and Goulden (2004) found that men, but not women, who received their doctorates between 1978 and 1984 benefited from having "early" babies (at least one child within five years of earning the doctorate) in terms of achieving tenure, regardless of academic discipline or institutional type. Specifically, the probability of men with early babies achieving tenure was 38 percent higher than for women with early babies after controlling for other variables. Women with early babies were also less likely than women without babies to hold a tenure-track faculty position after earning the doctorate. Most women (56 percent) who earned tenure within twelve years of receiving their doctorate did not have children in the household at any point after earning the doctorate, while most men (70 percent) who earned tenure within this period did have children.

Men, but not women, also appear to receive a salary premium from having children. Barbezat (1988) found that among national samples of faculty working at four-year institutions in 1968 and 1977, marital status was unrelated to the salaries of both women and men after controlling for education; experience; time spent on teaching, research, and administration; academic field; and publications. Having children was associated with higher salaries, net of other variables, for men but not for women (Barbezat, 1988).

Research using more recent samples of faculty (Bellas, 1992; Toutkoushian, 1998) shows a salary premium for marriage among men, but not among women, and suggests that men who have wives who are not employed receive even greater rewards. Using data from a 1984 Carnegie Foundation for the Advancement of Teaching survey of faculty and limiting the analyses to men, Bellas (1992) found that research productivity, rank, and salary were all higher for married men than for single men after controlling for education, experience, institutional characteristics, academic field, and time on research. While having a wife who was not employed did not add incremental benefit to married men in terms of research productivity or rank, having a wife who was not employed was associated with an additional salary premium. Specifically, married men received higher salaries than single men, and men with nonemployed wives received higher salaries than men with employed wives.

Similarly, using data from the NSOPF:93 and controlling for education, experience, academic field, publications, and institutional characteristics, Toutkoushian (1998) found that average salaries were 4 to 9 percent higher (depending on the variables that were controlled) for married men than for single men faculty employed at four-year colleges and universities in fall 1992. Marital status was unrelated to salaries for women faculty, net of other variables.

Research consistently shows that married faculty are not less productive than single faculty after controlling for other variables. In her review and synthesis of prior research, Creamer (1998) concluded that most research shows no relationship between marital status and publishing productivity for women. Some evidence suggests that married faculty are more productive than other faculty after controlling for other differences (Bellas, 1992; Bellas and Toutkoushian, 1999). Using data from the NSOPF:93 and limiting the analyses to full-time faculty with an academic rank of lecturer or higher, Bellas and Toutkoushian (1999) found that research productivity, measured by the number of various types of publications, was higher for married faculty than for other faculty after controlling for educational attainment, experience, allocation of time, institutional type, rank, and academic field.

The relationship between parental responsibilities and research productivity is ambiguous. In her review of ten studies, Creamer (1998) found no significant relationship between having children and publishing productivity in five studies, a positive relationship in three studies, and a negative relationship in two studies. Bellas and Toutkoushian (1999) showed that among full-time faculty with academic rank who were employed at two-year and four-year colleges nationwide in fall 1992, those with dependents had higher levels of research productivity than those without dependents after controlling for differences in other variables.

Although research generally suggests that being married and having children is associated with better employment outcomes for men but not women faculty, our understanding of the relationships is limited in several respects. First, little is known about the extent to which perceptions about the challenges of achieving both work and family outcomes influence decisions to pursue faculty careers. With some exceptions (for example, Mason and Goulden, 2004; Wolfinger, Mason, and Goulden, 2004), quantitative studies typically use cross-sectional databases such as the NSOPF:93 and NSOPF:99. These data sets, sponsored by the National Center for Education Statistics, have several strengths, including large samples of faculty from all types of nonprofit colleges and universities, high response rates, and variables describing a large number of faculty characteristics and experiences. Nonetheless, by definition, analyses of cross-sectional samples of faculty exclude individuals who have decided not to pursue faculty careers or who have left faculty careers because of perceived or actual work/family challenges. The National Science Foundation's Survey of Doctorate Recipients is a longitudinal database, tracking the demographic and career history of individuals over time. Nonetheless, this database also includes limited measures of family formation and attitudes.

Because the data were not collected specifically for examining work/family issues, quantitative analyses of the relationship between family and employment outcomes typically rely on a small number of variables (for example, married, yes or no; number of children) with little attention to the dimensions of family. Examples of potentially important variables that are not available in the National Center for Education Statistics or National Science Foundation databases include child care arrangements, income of the spouse, amount of time spent out of the labor force because of family responsibilities, and time devoted to household and caregiving. Little is also known about aspects of parent caregiving, another potentially important influence on employment status. A 1997 national survey of the wage and salaried labor force found that 25 percent of all workers had elder care responsibilities during the prior year, that employees with elder care responsibilities provided an average of eleven hours per week in assistance, and that 37 percent of employees with elder care responsibilities took time off from work to provide that assistance (Bond, Galinsky, and Swanberg, 1997). Finally, most research uses a traditional definition of marriage, with little attention to other relationships such as same-sex partnerships.

Reasons for the Relationship Between Family and Employment Outcomes

In part because of the tendency to use cross-sectional rather than longitudinal data, the direction of causality between family outcomes (for example, marriage, children) and employment outcomes is ambiguous. In other words, are family outcomes a cause or a consequence of employment outcomes? Economic perspectives predict that family commitments are a cause of employment outcomes. Other perspectives (Drago and Colbeck, 2003) suggest that structural and social forces restrict the extent to which faculty can achieve both work and family, thus requiring faculty to choose between family and employment outcomes.

Toutkoushian (1998) argues that sex differences in the relationship between family responsibilities and such employment outcomes as salaries may reflect the economic forces of supply and demand. In terms of supply-side forces, married women and women with children may achieve lower employment outcomes than men because women are more likely than men to devote less time to work than to their families or to place greater priority on their husband's career than their own, or both. In terms of demand-side forces, women may receive lower salaries than men because men, as the primary breadwinners, are more sensitive to salaries than women are (Toutkoushian, 1998).

Perna (2001, 2005) also draws on an economic perspective to frame her examinations of the relationship between family and employment outcomes. According to the economic theory of human capital, an individual's status and rewards in the academic labor market are determined primarily by his or her productivity. Productivity is expected to be determined by the investments that individuals make in themselves, particularly the quantity and quality of their education and the amount of their on-the-job training, as well as their geographical mobility, motivation and intensity of work, and emotional and physical health (Becker, 1962, 1993).

An economic perspective suggests that family commitments influence investment in human capital, continuity of labor force participation, types of employment sought, and level of commitment to the job (Becker, 1985; Polachek, 1977). An individual who is out of the labor force because of family commitments is not acquiring additional on-the-job experience and may even be losing some previously acquired job skills, thereby reducing the accumulation of human capital (Becker, 1993). Research shows that women are less mobile than men, suggesting that family commitments reduce geographical mobility (Marwell, Rosenfeld, and Spilerman, 1979; Rosenfeld and Jones, 1987). Family commitments may also be related to the level of motivation and intensity of work. Human capital theorists (such as Becker, 1985) predict that compared with men and single women, married women pursue less demanding jobs, such as part-time and non-tenure-track positions, because family responsibilities require more effort than leisure and other nonmarket activities and, consequently, they have less energy available for market work. Marriage and parenting may also influence emotional and physical health, as research shows that child care and other household responsibilities are a greater source of stress for women than for men faculty and that women perceive more conflict between work and family demands than men do (Austin and Pilat, 1990; Dey, 1994; Sorcinelli and Near, 1989; Tack and Patitu, 1992).

Nonetheless, as Perna (2001, 2005) notes and as the research that is summarized above suggests, research provides inconsistent support for economic claims about the relationship between family and such employment outcomes as tenure, rank, and salaries. Multivariate analyses suggest that marital and parental status are associated with a benefit to the employment outcomes of men faculty. While marriage may impose a cost on women in terms of employment and tenure status (Mason and Goulden, 2004; Perna, 2001), marriage and parenting seem unrelated to such outcomes as rank and salaries among women faculty (Barbezat, 1988; Ferber and Hoffman, 1997; Perna, 2005; Toutkoushian, 1998; Wolfinger, Mason, and Goulden, 2004).

Emphasizing the roles of structural and social forces, Drago and Colbeck (2003) offer an alternative framework for understanding the relationship between family and employment outcomes among college and university faculty. Drago and Colbeck assert that three social forces—the ideal worker norm, the norm of motherhood, and sex discrimination—result in a "bias against caregiving" in U.S. colleges and universities. The ideal worker norm is the expectation that employees place the highest priority on their careers, with little time or energy directed toward family and other nonwork commitments. The norm of motherhood is the persisting societal perception that women should be the primary caregivers of their children. Sex discrimination describes differences in an institution's treatment of women and men.

Drago and Colbeck (2003) argue that the ideal worker norm and the norm of motherhood are incompatible, especially in the context of sex discrimination, resulting in a bias against caregiving. Workers typically respond to the bias against caregiving with "bias avoidance," with a smaller number of faculty responding with "bias resistance." Bias avoidance involves intentionally minimizing family commitments in order to enhance career outcomes. Such bias avoidance is "productive" if it enhances work performance and "unproductive" if it does not. Productive bias avoidance behaviors may include forgoing marriage or children and limiting the number of children. Unproductive bias avoidance includes such behaviors as not asking for needed assistance (such as a reduced teaching load or a stopped tenure clock), not bringing children to the office during school breaks, and returning to work too soon after the birth of a child. Bias resistance involves challenging the conflict between the ideal worker and motherhood norms by openly discussing family commitments in the workplace, pushing for policies and programs to assist faculty with managing work/family demands, and supporting faculty's nonwork commitments.

Barriers to Gender Equity in Family and Employment Outcomes

Further consideration of the Drago and Colbeck framework in the context of other research suggests that several barriers restrict the achievement of what Mason and Goulden (2004) label gender equity, defined as equity between women and men in terms of family and employment outcomes. Sex differences in preferences for marriage and family do not seem to be a primary cause of gender gaps in family outcomes. The higher rates of separation, divorce, and widowhood for women than for men that are described above suggest that faculty work imposes more risks to the marriages of women faculty than the marriages of men faculty. Using data from the Survey of Doctorate Recipients, Mason and Goulden (2004) found that among faculty who were married within three years of receiving their doctorates, ladder-rank women faculty were more likely than ladder-rank men faculty and "second-tier" women faculty (for example, women with non-tenure-track and part-time faculty positions, women who were not working) to be divorced twelve years after receiving the Ph.D. even after controlling for other variables.

Other data suggest that a larger share of women than men faculty have at least some regret attached to their decision to limit family commitments in order to conform to the ideal worker norm. Among ladder-rank faculty between the ages of thirty and fifty who were employed at University of California institutions, a higher percentage of women than men had fewer children than they wanted: 40 percent of women versus 20 percent of men (Mason and Goulden, 2004). A survey of tenure-line faculty in English and chemistry at institutions nationwide showed similar results: 36 percent of women and 13 percent of men reported having fewer than the desired number of children in order to achieve career goals (Drago and Colbeck, 2003). Both surveys also showed that a somewhat higher share of women than men reported staying single because of their careers: 11 percent of women versus 7 percent of men in Mason and Goulden (2004) and 16 percent of women and 10 percent of men in Drago and Colbeck.

Other research suggests that some women who want marriage and children settle for lower-status positions. Mason and Goulden (2004) found that twelve years after 1978–1983 doctoral recipients received their degrees, comparable shares of women in second-tier positions (for example, part-time faculty, non-tenure-track faculty, nonworking) and men in full-time tenured and tenure-track positions were married and had at least one child (60 percent versus 69 percent). But only 41 percent of women in full-time tenured and tenure-track positions were married with at least one child. Drago and Colbeck (2003) identified women with doctorates who did not enter the tenure track because of family concerns, concluding that at least some women appear to have accepted the career consequences that result from achieving family outcomes.

The Drago and Colbeck framework suggests that several structural and social forces contribute to the notion that family commitments come at the expense of career attainment among college and university faculty. These forces include the structural constraints that the tenure system imposes, societal perceptions of mothers who work, sex differences in household demands, and the activities perceived to be required of the "ideal worker."

Achieving gender equity requires recognizing and addressing the structural constraints that are imposed by the tenure system (Drago and

Colbeck, 2003). For women, the tenure and biological clocks typically tick simultaneously. Based on their assessment of the average age of women assistant professors in the context of biological constraints on childbearing, Jacobs and Winslow (2003) concluded that most women faculty are too old to wait until after they have earned tenure to have a baby. But Mason and Goulden (2004) showed that not waiting until tenure is achieved to have a baby may jeopardize a woman's ability to earn tenure, as tenure rates are lower for women with "early babies" than for men with "early babies." Likely in part because of this catch-22, women who assume ladder-rank faculty positions are less likely than both ladder-rank men and second-tier women to be married or have a child under the age of six within three years of earning the doctorate (Mason and Goulden, 2004). Among those who were not married or were without children under the age of six within three years of receiving the doctorate, ladder-rank women faculty were less likely than ladder-rank men and second-tier women to subsequently marry or have a child under the age of six enter the household within twelve years of receiving the doctorate even after controlling for other variables (Mason and Goulden, 2004). Drago and Colbeck (2003) argued that the pressures of achieving tenure impose a structural bias against caregiving, thus encouraging such behaviors as timing children for either before starting a faculty career or after earning tenure, as well as staying single, forgoing children, or finding a partner who will assume childcare responsibilities. Although such behaviors may be "productive" in terms of promoting career attainment, they are likely to be unproductive in terms of promoting family outcomes.

Although the prevalence has declined, the norm of motherhood that Drago and Colbeck (2003) describe endures in American society. Data from surveys of workers in all industries shed light on broader societal perceptions of working mothers. Data from the National Study of the Changing Workforce, a periodic national survey of samples of approximately thirty-five hundred wage, salaried, and self-employed workers, suggest that the share of workers who believe that women should not enter the workforce has declined over the past twenty-five years, especially among men (Bond, Thompson, Galinsky, and Prottas, 2002). Despite this shift, however, more than one-third of all workers continue to believe that men should be employed and women should take care of the home and family. In 2002, 42 percent of men, and 37 percent of women, believed that women should stay at home while men earned the family's income, down from 74 percent of men and 52 percent of women in 1977. In 2002, about one-third (36 percent) of men and one-fifth (22 percent) of women workers believed that mothers who work do not have as good a relationship with their children as do mothers not working outside the home. The multifaceted examination of work/family commitments among tenure-line faculty in English and chemistry by Drago and Colbeck (2003) shows the continued applicability of the norm of motherhood to faculty. Among their findings is the notion of "daddy privilege," wherein fathers are praised when family commitments encroach on work demands but mothers in similar situations are subject to bias against caregiving.

Societal perceptions of the appropriate roles of women and men are not limited to caregiving responsibilities but extend to household management. One likely explanation for why men, but not women, benefit from having children in terms of such outcomes as tenure, rank, productivity, and salary pertains to sex differences in the distribution of household responsibilities. Using 1990 census data, Jacobs and Winslow (2003) showed that among married faculty, a higher share of women than men had a spouse who worked full time (89 percent versus 56 percent). Mason and Goulden (2004) found that among University of California faculty between the ages of thirty and fifty, women devoted more hours than men to both caregiving and household responsibilities. Women with children reported averaging thirty-six hours per week on caregiving, while men with children reported averaging twenty hours per week. Women averaged fifteen hours per week, and men averaged twelve hours per week, on housework.

Drago and Colbeck (2003) argued that faculty approach work and family, at least in part, in the context of the norm of the ideal worker. In U.S. higher education, the definition of the ideal worker seems to include working a high number of hours. Jacobs and Winslow (2003) observed that regardless of institutional type, tenure status, or rank, both women and men faculty averaged more than fifty hours of work per week. About 43 percent of men and 34 percent of women full-time faculty worked more than sixty hours each week. Mason and Goulden (2004) reported that among University of California faculty between the ages of thirty and fifty, women with children averaged 101 hours per week on work, caregiving, and household activities, while men with children averaged 88 hours per week. Arguing that self-reported time allocations may not reflect actual time expenditures, Drago and Colbeck (2003) shadowed thirteen tenured and tenure-track English and chemistry faculty at two large research universities. They found that faculty who spent more time on work also spent less time on child care. The five faculty who allocated the smallest share of their time to work (all women) also spent the most time caring for children. Other research suggests that faculty, especially women, make trade-offs in the expenditure of time not only between work and child care but also between work and leisure. In an exploratory study of 112 faculty in four departments at one university, Sorcinelli and Near (1989) found that job and life satisfaction were more closely related among faculty than among other workers. While about half of both women and men experienced stress in managing work and family commitments, a higher share of women than men experienced negative spillover of work into leisure, or the need to reduce leisure in order to satisfy work demands.

Recommendations for Institutional Policy and Practice

This research review suggests that in the context of current policies, practices, and social forces, most women faculty cannot have it all. In other words, the odds are currently against women achieving equity in terms of both family and employment outcomes. Institutional leaders should consider the consequences of policies, practices, and social forces that force women to choose between work and family by either forgoing family to achieve career success or by limiting the employment outcomes of faculty who want family commitments. Little is known about the extent to which the best and brightest forgo or leave an academic career because of the barriers described in this chapter. The declines in the representation of women at various points in the academic pipeline suggest leakage that may be attributable, at least in part, to the perceived incompatibility between work and family among faculty. In 2001, women received the majority of bachelor's degrees (57 percent) and master's degrees (59 percent), but fewer than half of doctoral degrees (45 percent). The pipeline leaks again between doctoral degree attainment and faculty employment, as women composed only 36 percent of all full-time faculty at degree-granting institutions nationwide in fall 1998 (U.S. Department of Education, 2003).

Chapters Three, Four, and Five in this volume describe the availability of work/family policies. These chapters, as well as other research (Finkel, Olswang, and She, 1994; Mason and Goulden, 2004; Raabe, 1997), demonstrate that establishing work/family policies is not enough. Faculty must also know about and use those policies.

Substantial percentages of faculty engage in behaviors that include not using, and not asking for, policies and programs that might enable them to meet both family and career commitments better. For example, in a survey of English and chemistry faculty at a sample of colleges and universities nationwide, Drago and Colbeck (2003) found that about one-third of both fathers and mothers did not request parental leave when they needed it and about one-fifth of fathers and mothers did not stop the tenure clock for a new child. About half (51 percent) of mothers reported returning to work too soon after childbirth.

Based on their work/family study, Drago and Colbeck offered a series of recommendations for faculty, department heads, and institutions. Their recommendations are designed to encourage more inclusive practices—practices that not only recognize that faculty have work commitments, but also encourage implementation and use of policies that minimize institutional bias against caregiving (such as tenure clock stoppage, parental leave, load reductions, and child care).

Research suggests that by implementing work/family policies, institutions may reduce the tendency of faculty to engage in behaviors that not only do not enhance work performance but also diminish family outcomes (Drago and Colbeck, 2003). Drago and Colbeck found that as the number of work/family policies at an institution increases, so does the tendency of faculty to take advantage of such policies. Institutions that are responsive to family concerns are characterized not only by lower bias avoidance but also by higher recruitment and retention of women faculty and higher rates of faculty child rearing.

In addition to promoting the use of policies and practices that are explicitly designed to help faculty manage both career and family demands (such as stopping the tenure clock), institutional leaders should also encourage a redefinition of the "ideal worker." As suggested by tenure requirements and faculty work habits, the ideal worker is now typically defined in terms of quantity: the number of hours worked, the number of journal articles produced, the number of grants received. Given that time is finite and that achieving family commitments also requires time, perceptions of the ideal worker that are based even in part on time are a substantial barrier to achieving gender equity in family and career outcomes. Redefining the ideal worker to emphasize quality of output rather than quantity of time invested would not only be a more useful measure of faculty work performance but also may reduce the gender inequities in faculty family and employment outcomes.

Institutions should also encourage faculty to take advantage of work/family policies. As Drago and Colbeck (2003) caution, use of productive bias avoidance behaviors, such as staying single, forgoing children, and timing children for after tenure, lessens the perceived demand for work/family policies. These behaviors may promote gender equity in career outcomes but not in terms of family outcomes. Moreover, such behaviors also sustain a culture in which family commitments are minimized, perpetuating the belief that family commitments are incompatible with career success. A more effective approach to achieving gender equity in both family and employment may be for more faculty, both women and men, to engage in the bias resistance that Drago and Colbeck described. Rather than minimizing family commitments through intentional strategies (such as staying single) or by hiding them (such as not stopping the tenure clock when needed), bias resistance requires explicitly addressing the conflicts between work and family commitments. Institutional leaders at all levels, from department chair to president, may promote greater gender equity in family outcomes through positive responses to such behaviors.

In summary, although progress has been made in increasing gender equity in faculty representation, substantially more progress is needed with regard to gender equity in both family and employment outcomes. The research and frameworks described in this chapter should assist institutional leaders in understanding the magnitude and dimensions of the problem.

References

Austin, A. E., and Pilat, M. "Tension, Stress, and the Tapestry of Faculty Lives." *Academe,* 1990, *77,* 38–42.

Barbezat, D. A. "Gender Differences in the Academic Reward System." In D. W. Breneman and T.I.K. Youn (eds.), *Academic Labor Markets and Careers.* Bristol, Pa.: Falmer Press, 1988.

Becker, G. S. "Investment in Human Capital: A Theoretical Analysis." *Journal of Political Economy,* 1962, *70*(Suppl. 5), 9–49.

Becker, G. S. "Human Capital, Effort, and the Sexual Division of Labor." *Journal of Labor Economics,* 1985, *3*(1), S33-S58.

Becker, G. S. *Human Capital.* Chicago: University of Chicago Press, 1993.

Bellas, M. L. "The Effects of Marital Status and Wives' Employment on the Salaries of Faculty Men: The (House) Wife Bonus." *Gender and Society,* 1992, *6,* 609–622.

Bellas, M. L., and Toutkoushian, R. K. "Faculty Time Allocations and Research Productivity: Gender, Race, and Family Effects." *Review of Higher Education,* 1999, *22,* 367–390.

Bond, J. T., Galinsky, E., and Swanberg, J. E. *The 1997 National Study of the Changing Workforce.* New York: Families and Work Institute, 1997.

Bond, J. T., Thompson, C., Galinsky, E., and Prottas, D. *Highlights of the National Study of the Changing Workforce.* New York: Families and Work Institute, 2002.

Bradburn, E. M., and Sikora, A. C. *Gender and Racial/Ethnic Differences in Salary and Other Characteristics of Postsecondary Faculty: Fall 1998.* NCES 2002–170. Washington, D.C.: U.S. Department of Education, National Center for Education Statistics, 2002.

Creamer, E. G. *Assessing Faculty Publication Productivity: Issues of Equity.* ASHE-ERIC Higher Education Report, Vol. 26, no. 2. Washington, D.C.: George Washington University, Graduate School of Education and Human Development, 1998.

Dey, E. L. "Dimensions of Faculty Stress: A Recent Survey." *Review of Higher Education,* 1994, *17,* 305–322.

Drago, R., and Colbeck, C. *The Mapping Project: Exploring the Terrain of U.S. Colleges and Universities for Faculty and Families: Final Report for the Alfred P. Sloan Foundation.* University Park: Pennsylvania State University, 2003. http://lsir.la.psu.edu/work-fam/mappingproject.htm.

Ferber, M. A., and Hoffman, E. P. "Are Academic Partners at a Disadvantage?" In M. A. Ferber and J. W. Loeb (eds.), *Academic Couples: Problems and Promises.* Chicago: University of Illinois Press, 1997.

Finkel, S. K., Olswang, S., and She, N. "Childbirth, Tenure, and Promotion for Women Faculty." *Review of Higher Education,* 1994, *17,* 259–270.

Jacobs, J. A., and Winslow, S. E. "The Academic Life Course: Time Pressures and Gender Inequality." Paper presented at " 'Mommies' and 'Daddies' on the 'Fast Track': Success of Parents in Demanding Professions," Alice Paul Center for Research on Women and Gender, University of Pennsylvania, Philadelphia, 2003.

Marwell, G., Rosenfeld, R., and Spilerman, S. "Geographic Constraints on Women's Careers in Academia." *Science,* 1979, *205,* 1225–1231.

Mason, M. A., and Goulden, M. "Marriage and Baby Blues: Re-Defining Gender Equity in the Academy." *Annals of the American Academy of Political and Social Science,* 2004, *596,* 86–103.

Parsad, B., and Glover, D. *Tenure Status of Postsecondary Instructional Faculty and Staff: 1992–98.* NCES 2002–110. Washington, D.C.: U.S. Department of Education, National Center for Education Statistics, 2002.

Perna, L. W. "The Relationship Between Family Responsibilities and Employment Status Among College and University Faculty." *Journal of Higher Education,* 2001, *72,* 584–611.

Perna, L. W. "Sex Differences in Faculty Tenure and Promotion: The Contribution of Family Ties." *Research in Higher Education,* 2005, *46*(3), 277–307.

Polachek, S. W. "Occupational Segregation Among Women: Theory, Evidence, and a Prognosis." In C. B. Lloyd, E. S. Andrews, and C. L. Gilroy (eds.), *Women in the Labor Market.* New York: Columbia University Press, 1977.

Raabe, P. H. "Work/Family Policies for Faculty: How 'Career- and Family-Friendly' Is Academe?" In M. A. Ferber and J. W. Loeb (eds.), *Academic Couples: Problems and Promises.* Urbana: University of Illinois Press, 1997.

Rosenfeld, R. A., and Jones, J. A. "Patterns and Effects of Geographic Mobility for Academic Women and Men." *Journal of Higher Education,* 1987, *58,* 493–515.

Rubley, J. N. "Job Sharing on the Tenure Track: To Make Time for Their Children, Two Academics Opt to Share a Faculty Position and a Half." *Chronicle of Higher Education,* Feb. 6, 2004, p. C2.

Sorcinelli, M. D., and Near, J. P. "Relations Between Work and Life Away from Work Among University Faculty." *Journal of Higher Education,* 1989, *60,* 59–81.

Tack, M. W., and Patitu, C. L. *Faculty Job Satisfaction: Women and Minorities in Peril.* ASHE-ERIC Higher Education Report, no. 4. Washington, D.C.: George Washington University, School of Education and Human Development, 1992.

Toutkoushian, R. K. "Racial and Marital Status Differences in Faculty Pay." *Journal of Higher Education,* 1998, *69*(5), 513–541.

U.S. Department of Education. *Digest of Education Statistics 2002.* Washington, D.C.: National Center for Education Statistics, 2003.

Williams, J. C. "Singing the Babies Blues: If Having Children on the Tenure Track Is a Career Killer, Is Having Them in Graduate School Any Better?" *Chronicle of Higher Education,* Apr. 23, 2004, p. C2.

Wilson, R. "How Babies Alter Careers: Having Children Often Bumps Women off the Tenure Track, a New Study Shows." *Chronicle of Higher Education,* Dec. 5, 2003, p. A1.

Wolfinger, N. H., Mason, M. A., and Goulden, M. "Problems in the Pipeline: Gender, Marriage, and Fertility in the Ivory Tower." Paper presented at the annual meeting of the American Sociological Association, San Francisco, Aug. 2004.

LAURA PERNA is assistant professor in the Department of Education Policy and Leadership at the University of Maryland, College Park.

2

If career experiences of women academics are significantly different from those of men, analysts of gender equity need to take those differences into account.

Career Paths for Women Faculty: Evidence from NSOPF:99

Valerie Martin Conley

It is generally accepted that women have more varied career paths to and through academe than men do. One of the commonly cited reasons for these circuitous paths is that women bear more of the responsibility for family caretaking than men do. Regardless of the inroads women have made in the professional labor force since World War II, there is still substantial evidence to suggest that at least for scientists and engineers, marriage and family affect men and women's careers differently (Long, 2001). Even in situations where women are not focusing priorities on family, the perception prevails that they are or will be, and barriers may exist that impose societal expectations on women relative to childbearing, child care, and coordinating with a husband's career. Women may be more likely to postpone graduate school or make conservative decisions regarding choice of graduate school or first appointment, leading to an unintended consequence that is well documented: differential career progress, particularly in prestigious research institutions (Clark and Corcoran, 1986).

Career disruption may also contribute to differential progress. Scholars have examined the relationship between gender, career disruption, and academic rewards in specific disciplines. For example, McElrath (1992) studied faculty in criminology and sociology, and Reagan (1975) provided a report of the Committee on the Status of Women in the Economics Profession. In both disciplines, women were more likely to interrupt their careers than men were. Furthermore, McElrath (1992) found substantial effects on tenure when women interrupted their careers, including a decrease in the probability of obtaining tenure and an increase in the length

NEW DIRECTIONS FOR HIGHER EDUCATION, no. 130, Summer 2005 © Wiley Periodicals, Inc.

of time to attain it. Pregnancy, child rearing, and furthering the career of a job-seeking spouse were among the reasons for interrupting careers.

This chapter uses data from the 1999 National Study of Postsecondary Faculty (NSOPF: 99) to explore the education and employment histories of women faculty and examine differences between women and men across different stages of their careers.

Characteristics of Women Faculty

Of the approximately 975,000 instructional faculty and staff nationwide in fall 1998, about 40 percent were women. There was an even split among women by employment status. About half were employed full time (51 percent) and half part time (49 percent). In contrast, the majority of men were employed in full-time positions (62 percent). The substantial presence of women among part-time faculty is well documented (Conley and Leslie, 2002; Perna, 2001). Among the reasons often cited for the prevalence of women in part-time academic positions is that a smaller percentage of women than men faculty members (36 versus 59 percent) have attained a doctorate or first professional degree. However, it is also the case that women tend to be employed in public two-year institutions where the doctorate is not as often a prerequisite for employment. It stands to reason that faculty credentials would be tied to the highest degree conferred at the institution where the faculty member is employed. Unfortunately, this is usually where the discussion ends, primarily because there is insufficient evidence to determine whether women are filling these positions by choice or are somehow being tracked into them. Analysis of motives for part-time employment is far from definitive, since responses to two NSOPF:99 survey questions on this issue are ambiguous. The questions ask whether faculty were employed in part-time positions because they preferred working part time and whether they were working part time because full-time employment was unavailable. (These two items were not mutually exclusive.) Responses suggest that more men than women prefer part-time employment, and there was no statistically significant difference between men and women working part time because full-time employment was unavailable (Conley and Leslie, 2002).

At a minimum, it is important to recognize that part-time faculty careers are different from full-time faculty careers. It is also important to recognize that faculty careers are different in four-year institutions than in two-year institutions. Indeed, a terminal degree is often a requirement for a faculty position in four-year institutions, and the majority of instructional faculty employed full time in four-year institutions held a doctorate or first professional degree in the fall of 1998 (83 percent of men and 68 percent of women). Doctoral and first professional degrees are not the only degrees recognized as terminal degrees, however. A higher percentage of women than men (5 percent versus 3 percent) held terminal master's degrees (for example, M.F.A., M.S.W.). Yet a clear majority of terminal degrees are at the doctoral level. The number and percentage of women attaining the doctoral degree has been increasing steadily, albeit slowly, over time. Forty-five percent of all doctoral degrees conferred in academic year 2000–2001 were awarded to women, a significant increase from approximately 10 percent of doctorates in the early 1900s and 31 percent in 1980–1981 (U.S. Department of Education, 2003).

Although the number of doctoral degrees conferred on women has been increasing, the pattern of employment of women in prestigious research institutions is not so clear-cut. Over the six-year period between the fall of 1992 and the fall of 1998, the percentage of female faculty who taught full time in public research institutions increased from 23 percent to 30 percent, but the percentage teaching in private research institutions decreased from 31 percent to 26 percent (Glover and Parsad, 2002). In fact, the analyses indicated that most of the changes in gender composition occurred in public institutions. The percentage of female faculty who taught full time in public institutions increased from 34 percent to 37 percent between the fall of 1992 and the fall of 1998.

When academic discipline is taken into account, full-time women faculty members are still more prevalent in certain fields. Women were more proportionately represented in education, the humanities, and health sciences. Forty-one percent of humanities faculty members were women, as were 42 percent of health sciences faculty members. Two disciplines, English and nursing, comprise the bulk of women in these two program areas.

There is also a persistent gender gap in tenure status among full-time instructional faculty and staff (Parsad and Glover, 2002). Not only are full-time male faculty more likely to be tenured, but men have held tenure longer than women on average. Sixty percent of male faculty and 42 percent of female faculty reported that they had tenure in the fall of 1998. In addition, opportunities for becoming tenured for all faculty members have been steadily declining as the percentage of faculty on tenure track decreases and the percentage of faculty hired full time off the tenure track increases. The next section explores potential reasons for these persistent gaps, including the concept of accumulative disadvantage and barriers to career advancement.

Accumulative Disadvantage

Clark and Corcoran (1986) analyzed the relationship between academic preparation and career success by conducting interviews with 147 faculty members in the biological sciences, physical sciences and mathematics, social sciences, and humanities. Specifically, they explored the concept of "accumulative disadvantage" and concluded that although a critical mass of women may now hold academic positions, their career success may be limited. Women's careers are hampered by practices and processes that continue to perpetuate inequities and the marginality of their careers relative to those of men. Clark and Corcoran found that women academics had difficulties in overcoming cultural barriers to entering academic careers, had advisers who doubted their potential for engaging in productive research, and faced structural impediments to success such as opportunities to participate fully in the collegial culture and networks leading to more prestigious positions. The researchers refer to these experiences as the "triple penalty" and conclude that while women may no longer be excluded from academe outright, the accumulative disadvantage may limit potential career success:

> If women do not enroll in the best graduate programs, do not receive parity in financial aids, do not become protégés of productive, established academicians, do not have resources to carry out their research and scholarly work, do not penetrate the collegial networks where useful advice, advocacy, and patronage are dispensed, and so forth, they may begin with initial disadvantage and find that it grows with time. When they are reviewed for tenure and promotion, their publication records may be inferior to those of men; in turn, if they have not accomplished much research, the funding gatekeepers may decide that there is little justification for granting financial support since the record of accomplishment is marginal [p. 24].

More recently, Bain and Cummings (2000) explored societal, professional-organizational, and institutional barriers to the career advancement of academic women. They point to two lines of inquiry that have developed to attempt to explain the scarcity of women in positions with the highest levels of power and prestige: societal barriers and professional-organizational barriers to career advancement. They add a third type of barrier, institutional traditions, which captures the notion that specific groups of academic systems share patterns that may influence the opportunities of women for advancement. Their description suggests a merged concept of structural stratification in women faculty members' careers, based on institution type and cultural influences through history and tradition. Others (see Chapter One, this volume, for example) have suggested barriers may be defined using the theoretical constructs of social and human capital. The purpose of this chapter is to look at career paths of women faculty using evidence from NSOPF:99.

Faculty Careers

Determinants of faculty careers and the paths research-oriented faculty have taken historically in the United States have been well documented (Wilson, 1942; Caplow and McGee, 1958; Finkelstein, 1984; Burke, 1988). Entry into the professoriate at prestigious research institutions (commonly understood as the top tier of American higher education) is generally determined by factors such as the prestige of the doctoral granting institution, department, and mentors.

Baldwin (1979) identified five stages of the faculty career: the assistant professor in the first three years of college teaching, the assistant professor beyond the first three years of college teaching, the associate professor, the continuing full professor, and the retiring professor. Lawrence (1998) distinguishes between career and career course. She defines *career* as "the set of hierarchically ordered and professionally relevant positions within a field or discipline in which entrance and progression are regulated by peers" (p. 19). *Career course* "refers to the configuration of activities and positions that characterize an individual within a field or profession" (p. 19). Most research on academic careers focuses on one of three stages: early career or novice, midcareer, and late career or senior (Baldwin and Blackburn, 1981; Bland and Bergquist, 1997). The three stages are derived from key developmental frameworks that describe successive stages of the professorial career. However, with the possible exception of the early or novice stage, little attention has been paid to the potential differences between women and men in each of the career stages.

Acknowledging as Lawrence (1998) did that careers are "situated in multiple contexts" (p. 27) and that women may take circuitous routes to and through academe, I will measure career stage using categories for early, mid-, and late career based on the respondent's current age. Early career faculty in this analysis includes individuals up to 40 years of age. I chose 40 as the cut-off for early career because the median age of doctorate recipients was 33.6 years in 2000. I then added six years to allow for a full tenure clock. I chose 55 as the cut-off for late career because it is the minimum age faculty may be eligible to retire under some plans. Thus, I chose 41 to 54 as the age range for midcareer (this age range, using the median age of doctorate recipients in 2000 again as a base, should allow sufficient time in rank for faculty members' promotion to full professor).

Evidence from NSOPF:99. Using this measure, one-quarter of full-time women faculty members were in the early stages of their careers, 53 percent were in midcareer, and 22 percent were in late career. The distributions of women across career stage were generally similar regardless of type and control of institution. Almost one third (32 percent) of tenured women faculty and two-fifths (42 percent) of full professor women faculty were in the late stages of their careers. If all 64 percent of the women associate professors in midcareer were promoted to full professor, an estimated 28,928 women would attain senior rank. However, if just half of the women faculty who currently hold full professor rank retired, the net gain would only be approximately 13,500, or about 2 percent of all full-time faculty members. The average age of men assistant, associate, and full professors was forty-two, fifty, and fifty-six years old, respectively, while the comparable ages for women were forty-four, fifty, and fifty-four (data not shown in tables).

Several items on the survey instrument were designed to gather information regarding the experiences and credentials of participants. Specifically, respondents were asked to complete information about each of their four highest degrees: the level of the degree, the field for each degree, and the institution from which they received each degree. Respondents were also asked about the first professional position they held in a higher education institution: number of years they held the job, type of institution, employment status of the position (full time or part time), academic rank when they began the position and when they left the position, and tenure status when they began the position and when they left the position. In addition, respondents were asked to indicate the total number of professional positions in higher education institutions that they had held. Finally, respondents were asked about professional positions they had held outside higher education institutions. Selected data on these characteristics will be provided for faculty in early, middle, and late stages of their career in three distinct clusters: full-time faculty in four-year institutions, full-time faculty in two-year institutions, and part-time faculty.

Table 2.1 shows selected characteristics of women faculty by career stage (current age). Men made up a higher percentage of full-time faculty members in each career stage than did women. However, the differences in the percentages of men and women were smaller for faculty in early and midcareer than late career. These data support the conjecture that institutions have been making some headway in filling vacant positions with women faculty and that more opportunities to diversify the faculty may be on the horizon as older faculty (the majority of them male) decide to retire.

For part-time faculty, a different pattern emerged. While a higher percentage of early career faculty members were women than were men, the reverse was true for part-time faculty in late career. Sixty-three percent of part-time faculty members in late career were male, leaving only 37 percent female.

Education and Employment History. Tables 2.2 through 2.4 show selected academic and employment characteristics of the first professional position in a higher education institution for men and women by career stage. The three tables provide information for full-time faculty in four-year institutions, full-time faculty in two-year institutions, and part-time faculty, respectively. Although NSOPF:99 does not contain explicit measures of prestige of the doctoral institution, department, and mentors, it does include the Carnegie classification of the doctoral degree institution. This measure will be used as a rough approximation of prestige.

In four-year institutions (Table 2.2), a higher percentage of full-time faculty members with doctorates were male than were female, regardless of career stage. However, consistent with data indicating that more women are attaining doctoral degrees, the differences in percentages of male and female are smaller for faculty in early career than in mid- and late career. A similar relationship exists for faculty with first-professional degrees. In two-year institutions (Table 2.3), the difference between the percentage of men and women in early and midcareer holding doctoral degrees was smaller than for faculty in four-year institutions.

For both men and women, employment status of the first higher education position appears related to the employment status of the current

Table 2.1. Selected Characteristics of Faculty by Career Stage, Fall 1998

	Early Career		Midcareer		Late Career	
	Men	Women	Men	Women	Men	Women
Employment status						
Part time	46.7	53.3	49.2	50.8	62.5	37.5
Full time	57.4	42.7	59.5	40.5	74.3	25.7
Institutional sector						
Four-year	54.6	45.4	59.0	41.0	72.7	27.3
Two-year	46.3	53.7	46.4	53.6	61.4	38.7
Institutional classification						
Public research	58.5	41.5	64.3	35.7	79.1	20.9
Private research	63.9	36.1	63.6	36.4	82.3	17.7
Public doctoral[a]	57.5	42.5	55.9	44.1	74.7	25.3
Private doctoral[a]	59.0	41.0	59.3	40.8	67.3	32.7
Public comprehensive	46.3	53.7	53.6	46.4	64.7	35.3
Private comprehensive	51.9	48.2	57.8	42.2	73.5	26.5
Private liberal arts	46.1	54.0	54.0	46.0	63.5	36.5
Public two year	46.8	53.2	46.7	53.3	63.0	37.0
Other	55.1	44.9	60.9	39.1	66.1	33.9
Faculty rank						
Full professor	63.2	36.8	73.7	26.3	83.6	16.4
Associate professor	67.2	32.8	64.9	35.1	70.0	30.0
Assistant professor	59.1	40.9	49.7	50.3	56.1	43.9
Other/NA/no rank	45.8	54.2	46.2	53.8	58.4	41.6
Tenure status						
Tenured	64.6	35.4	65.4	34.6	79.2	20.9
On tenure track	59.2	40.8	57.5	42.5	56.5	43.5
Not on tenure track	47.6	52.5	48.2	51.8	61.4	38.6
No tenure system	49.7	50.3	51.6	48.4	58.4	41.6
Highest degree						
Doctorate	61.1	38.9	64.8	35.3	78.3	21.7
First professional	65.0	35.0	72.8	27.3	88.2	11.8
Master's	44.3	55.7	42.9	57.1	56.2	43.8
Bachelor's	46.5	53.5	47.4	52.6	54.6	45.5

[a]Includes free-standing medical schools.

Source: U.S. Department of Education (n.d.).

position. Eighty-seven percent of men and 83 percent of women who were first employed full time were also currently employed full time. Similarly, 80 percent of men and women who were first employed part time were also currently employed part time. It is important to note that the NSOPF:99 data are retrospective, so faculty members in early and midcareer stages have naturally had less opportunity to change jobs than their more senior colleagues. However, less than one-quarter of faculty who reported their

**Table 2.2. Selected Academic and Employment Characteristics
of First Higher Education Position, by Gender and Career Stage:
Four Year, Full Time**

	Early Career		Midcareer		Late Career	
	Men	Women	Men	Women	Men	Women
Highest degree						
Doctorate	64.3	35.7	67.0	33.0	78.9	21.1
First professional	65.9	34.1	71.2	28.8	89.6	10.4
Master's	49.4	50.6	47.6	52.4	62.6	37.4
Bachelor's	54.1	45.9	50.1	49.9	76.3	23.7
Highest degree institution[a]						
Research I	62.3	37.7	67.5	32.5	81.2	18.8
Research II	65.6	34.4	68.7	31.3	79.8	20.2
Doctoral I	63.4	36.6	54.7	45.3	66.5	33.5
Doctoral II	53.1	46.9	63.1	36.9	73.5	26.5
Other/unknown	73.5	26.5	73.1	26.9	83.1	16.9
First Higher Education Position						
Employment status						
Full time	62.2	37.9	65.2	34.8	78.9	21.1
Part time	52.9	47.1	50.7	49.3	63.6	36.4
Sector						
Four-year doctoral	64.0	36.0	65.0	35.0	80.0	20.0
Four-year nondoctoral	54.5	45.5	61.0	39.0	73.5	26.5
Two year	37.7	62.3	54.4	45.6	60.9	39.1
Tenure status at hire						
Tenured	—	—	62.5	37.5	89.0	11.0
On tenure track	62.0	38.0	67.5	32.5	83.1	16.9
Not on tenure track	59.5	40.5	60.2	39.8	68.9	31.1
Employment history						
No previous employment	59.2	40.8	65.5	34.5	86.8	13.2
Only higher education	68.2	31.8	71.0	29.0	78.9	21.1
Previously only outside higher education	55.7	44.3	54.5	45.5	77.0	23.0
Both	56.8	43.2	59.4	40.7	71.8	28.2

[a]Includes only faculty with a Ph.D. or first professional degree.

Source: U.S. Department of Education (n.d.).

first position in higher education was part time were currently employed full time regardless of career stage (data not shown in tables). Table 2.4 gives the distribution of employment status of the first higher education position for faculty currently employed part time. More than half of faculty members in the early stages of their career whose first employment was full time, but are currently employed part time, were women (56 percent). These data may suggest that some women are reducing their work responsibilities in order to start a family.

Table 2.3. Selected Academic and Employment Characteristics of First Higher Education Position, by Gender and Career Stage: Two Year, Full Time

	Early Career		Midcareer		Late Career	
	Men	Women	Men	Women	Men	Women
Highest degree						
Doctorate	55.1	44.9	52.6	47.4	72.2	27.8
First professional	—	—	—	—	—	—
Master's	35.8	64.2	41.0	59.0	58.5	41.6
Bachelor's	38.0	62.0	45.5	54.5	56.4	43.6
Highest degree institution[a]						
Research I	55.6	44.5	58.9	41.1	74.0	26.0
Research II	—	—	40.7	59.3	—	—
Doctoral I	—	—	—	—	—	—
Doctoral II	—	—	—	—	—	—
Other/unknown	—	—	49.3	50.7	—	—
First Higher Education Position						
Employment status						
Full time	41.7	58.3	47.4	52.6	63.7	36.3
Part time	37.4	62.6	37.3	62.7	54.0	46.0
Sector						
Four-year doctoral	46.1	53.9	40.4	59.6	68.0	32.0
Four-year nondoctoral	26.3	73.7	41.5	58.5	59.8	40.2
Two-year	42.3	57.7	47.3	52.7	62.0	38.0
Tenure status at hire						
Tenured	—	—	54.9	45.2	64.4	35.7
On tenure track	42.2	57.8	47.5	52.5	66.6	33.4
Not on tenure track	40.9	59.1	42.9	57.1	59.3	40.7
Employment history						
No previous employment	39.1	61.0	53.2	46.8	61.2	38.8
Only higher education	44.0	56.0	44.7	55.4	65.9	34.1
Previously only outside higher education	38.3	61.7	49.8	50.2	64.4	35.7
Both	40.5	59.5	39.2	60.8	59.2	40.8

[a]Includes only faculty with a Ph.D. or first professional degree.

Source: U.S. Department of Education (n.d.).

Table 2.5 shows the percentage distribution of male and female faculty employed full time by career stage, highest-degree institution type, and current institution type. Forty-eight percent of early career men and 38 percent of early career women faculty members who graduated from a Research I institution with doctorates or first-professional degrees were currently employed in Research I institutions in the fall of 1998. This relationship was not as strong for other types of institutions, however. The majority of early

Table 2.4. Selected Academic and Employment Characteristics of First Higher Education Position, by Gender and Career Stage: Part Time

	Early Career		Midcareer		Late Career	
	Men	Women	Men	Women	Men	Women
Highest degree						
Doctorate	45.0	55.0	58.7	41.3	77.7	22.3
First professional	63.4	36.6	75.6	24.4	87.5	12.5
Master's	43.9	56.1	41.5	58.5	52.8	47.2
Bachelor's	46.9	53.1	47.6	52.4	50.2	49.8
Highest degree institution[a]						
Research I	58.5	41.5	61.3	38.8	80.9	19.1
Research II	—	—	52.6	47.4	77.9	22.1
Doctoral I	—	—	58.7	41.3	74.8	25.3
Doctoral II	—	—	55.1	44.9	—	—
Other/unknown	45.4	54.6	79.1	20.9	82.9	17.1
First Higher Education Position						
Employment status						
Full time	44.5	55.5	51.7	48.3	71.8	28.2
Part time	46.9	53.1	48.6	51.4	58.7	41.4
Sector						
Four-year doctoral	47.4	52.6	52.1	47.9	67.8	32.2
Four-year nondoctoral	48.4	51.6	50.1	49.9	57.2	42.8
Two-year	44.7	55.3	44.8	55.2	58.1	41.9
Tenure status at hire						
Tenured	—	—	—	—	68.6	31.5
On tenure track	52.1	47.9	56.7	43.3	82.4	17.6
Not on tenure track	46.6	53.4	48.6	51.4	58.7	41.4
Employment history						
No previous employment	52.8	47.2	51.9	48.1	64.8	35.2
Only higher education	41.5	58.5	45.5	54.6	64.5	35.5
Previously only outside higher education	47.0	53.0	44.5	55.5	59.2	40.8
Both	45.7	54.3	53.0	47.0	63.4	36.6

[a]Includes only faculty with a Ph.D. or first professional degree.

Source: U.S. Department of Education (n.d.).

career men who graduated from Research II institutions were employed in doctoral or comprehensive institutions in the fall of 1998, whereas the majority of early career women who graduated from Research II institutions were employed in comprehensive and liberal arts institutions. Regardless of career stage, women faculty who graduated from Research I institutions with doctorates or first professional degrees were less likely than their male counterparts to be employed in Research I institutions in the fall of 1998 (38 percent versus 48 percent, 36 percent versus 39 percent, and 30 percent versus 37 percent, respectively).

Table 2.5. **Percentage Distribution of Male and Female Faculty Employed Full Time, by Career Stage, Highest Degree Institution Type, and Current Institution Type**

	Employment Institutions (1994 Carnegie Classification)						
	Research I	Research II	Doctoral	Comprehensive	Liberal Arts	Two Year	Other
Highest degree institution, early career male							
Research I	47.5	8.6	14.8	13.5	8.8	3.1	3.7
Research II	9.1	12.9	23.0	38.1	7.2	7.5	2.2
Doctoral	12.8	8.8	20.3	25.3	19.2	12.0	1.6
Other	41.9	3.3	6.7	14.0	6.4	2.2	25.6
Highest degree institution, early career female							
Research I	38.0	7.7	14.6	20.1	11.9	4.0	3.8
Research II	7.9	8.5	9.2	35.6	33.0	5.9	0.0
Doctoral	8.4	12.7	25.0	31.0	6.8	8.6	7.6
Other	32.6	1.3	6.9	22.8	4.4	9.5	22.5
Highest degree institution, midcareer male							
Research I	39.1	9.5	10.9	19.5	11.0	4.0	6.0
Research II	22.6	12.6	10.7	33.3	12.3	6.1	2.5
Doctoral	7.0	7.6	16.7	31.6	18.7	9.6	9.0
Other	29.7	3.9	10.2	12.6	7.5	4.2	31.9
Highest degree institution, midcareer female							
Research I	35.8	6.7	11.2	24.5	9.6	5.7	6.6
Research II	11.5	14.5	7.5	32.8	9.7	17.1	6.9
Doctoral	12.8	2.7	24.3	27.2	15.9	9.0	8.2
Other	29.0	3.1	4.7	14.5	7.0	10.8	30.9
Highest degree institution, late career male							
Research I	36.6	8.1	13.1	23.4	8.0	4.8	6.0
Research II	12.4	17.6	11.0	33.3	13.2	8.8	3.7
Doctoral	16.7	3.5	13.8	30.7	18.3	10.6	6.6
Other	36.3	5.7	8.2	17.8	6.8	6.6	18.4
Highest degree institution, late career female							
Research I	29.6	4.9	11.6	34.8	8.1	7.1	3.9
Research II	6.9	14.0	11.9	35.2	15.0	11.6	5.5
Doctoral	10.0	8.3	20.4	33.8	13.9	9.5	4.2
Other	22.0	4.4	8.5	29.6	7.3	16.0	12.4

Note: Includes only faculty with a Ph.D. or first professional degree.

Source: U.S. Department of Education (n.d.).

Finally, the diagonals in Table 2.6 show that there is a relationship between the type of institution of first higher education employment and current employment for both men and women. (The diagonal cells in a table are those for which the row and column values are the same.) Fifty-four percent of late career women faculty members whose first higher education position was in a four-year doctoral granting institution were employed in that type of institution in the fall of 1998. An even greater percentage of older

Table 2.6. Percentage Distribution of Male and Female Faculty by Career Stage, Type of Institution of First Higher Education Position, and Current Employing Institution

	Current Institutional Classification		
	Four-Year Doctoral Granting	Four-Year Nondoctoral Granting	Two-Year
First higher education position, early career male			
Four-year doctoral granting	77.0	20.0	3.1
Four-year nondoctoral granting	16.0	80.5	3.5
Two-year	3.0	14.9	82.1
First higher education position, early career female			
Four-year doctoral granting	70.7	23.1	6.1
Four-year nondoctoral granting	13.9	75.2	10.9
Two-year	10.8	10.1	79.1
First higher education position, midcareer male			
Four-year doctoral granting	74.6	22.1	3.3
Four-year nondoctoral granting	18.9	74.6	6.6
Two-year	8.1	17.7	74.2
First higher education position, midcareer female			
Four-year doctoral granting	64.0	27.6	8.4
Four-year nondoctoral granting	18.3	68.3	13.4
Two-year	8.5	12.2	79.3
First higher education position, late career male			
Four-year doctoral granting	68.2	26.1	5.7
Four-year nondoctoral granting	20.7	71.3	8.0
Two-year	9.1	14.3	76.6
First higher education position, late career female			
Four-year doctoral granting	53.5	36.3	10.2
Four-year nondoctoral granting	18.7	67.3	14.0
Two-year	10.5	13.7	75.8

Source: U.S. Department of Education (n.d.).

women (67 percent) whose first higher education position was in a four-year nondoctoral granting institution were currently employed in the same type of institution. And 76 percent of older women whose first higher education position was in a two-year institution were currently employed in a two-year institution (Table 2.6). The comparable percentages for men were 68 percent in four-year doctoral-granting institutions, 71 percent in four-year non-doctoral-granting institutions, and 77 percent in two-year institutions. The NSOPF:99 survey did not include items that asked why faculty were employed in a particular type of institution, however, so it is not possible to determine whether the faculty member chose employment in a particular sector.

Number of Positions. On average, early career faculty had held two jobs and later career faculty had held three jobs (data not shown in tables). Multiple regression analyses indicate that being employed part time or off the tenure track in the first higher education position was related to the total number of positions held both inside and outside higher education during the course of a career (analyses are available from the author on request). Faculty who held their first position in higher education part time held more jobs on average than did those who were first employed full time. Conversely, faculty held significantly fewer positions overall (inside and outside of higher education) if their first higher education position was tenured or on the tenure track.

On average, late career women faculty held more jobs outside higher education than did late career men. This finding suggests that older women faculty, perhaps especially those educated at the top-tier institutions, may have sought career fulfillment outside higher education because of limited availability of employment opportunities within higher education. Another possible explanation may be that women were pulled away from higher education to accept more flexible work arrangements because of family responsibilities at some point during their careers.

Conclusion

In general, men and women appear to follow similar academic career paths. Statistically significant differences in the percentages of men and women with various characteristics at different career stages, however, suggest that some women may indeed be experiencing career paths somewhat different from men. NSOPF:99 provides only a glimpse into these differences because the survey has limited information on specific circumstances related to individual careers. Unfortunately, the survey does not include items that would allow researchers to directly test some of the hypotheses related to career interruption, cumulative disadvantage, or barriers to career advancement. For example, respondents are not asked whether they have ever interrupted their careers for family or other reasons or anything about their target or most desired job. Analysts must rely on a basic set of career status variables that allow us to look at two questions. First, for a given age, are women in comparable positions to men of the same age? And second, for a given age category, have men and women followed similar career paths? The available evidence is mixed on both. After taking highest degree and type of employing institution into account, there appear to be more similarities overall between the positions held by younger men and women than between older men and women. The increase in the percentage of doctoral degrees awarded to women and institutional efforts to diversify the faculty may be contributing to these observed patterns.

Analyses focused on gender may need to be expanded to take the full complement of potential circumstances into consideration, in addition to the traditional academic career path. These data suggest it may be plausible to consider whether some of the variables routinely used in analyses focused on gender, such as salary equity, may obscure some of the differences that exist. For example, if women are more likely to interrupt their careers or postpone or take longer to complete graduate school, what influence does measuring experience and awarding merit increases based on the number of years since highest degree have on their careers? Further research is needed that focuses more specifically on identifying and taking into account these potential systematic differences.

References

Bain, O., and Cummings, W. "Academe's Glass Ceiling: Societal, Professional-Organizational, and Institutional Barriers to the Career Advancement of Academic Women." *Comparative Education Review*, 2000, 29(4), 493–514.

Baldwin, R. *Adult Career Development: What Are the Implications for Faculty?* Washington, D.C.: American Association for Higher Education, 1979.

Baldwin, R., and Blackburn, R. T. "The Academic Career as a Developmental Process." *Journal of Higher Education*, 1981, 52, 598–619.

Bland, C. J., and Bergquist, W. H. *The Vitality of Senior Faculty Members: Snow on the Roof—Fire in the Furnace.* ASHE-ERIC Higher Education Report, Vol. 25, no. 7. Washington, D.C.: George Washington University, Graduate School of Education and Human Development, 1997.

Burke, D. L. *The New Academic Marketplace.* Westport, Conn.: Greenwood Press, 1988.

Caplow, T., and McGee, R. J. *The Academic Marketplace.* New York: Basic Books, 1958.

Clark, S. M., and Corcoran, M. "Perspectives on the Professional Socialization of Women Faculty: A Case of Accumulative Disadvantage?" *Journal of Higher Education*, 1986, 57(1), 20–43.

Conley, V. M., and Leslie, D. W. *Part-Time Instructional Faculty and Staff: Who They Are, What They Do, and What They Think.* NCES 2002–163. Washington, D.C.: National Center for Education Statistics, 2002.

Finkelstein, M. J. *The American Academic Profession: A Synthesis of Social Scientific Inquiry Since World War II.* Columbus: Ohio State University Press, 1984.

Glover, D., and Parsad, B. *The Gender and Racial/Ethnic Composition of Postsecondary Instructional Faculty and Staff, 1992–98.* NCES 2002–160. Washington, D.C.: National Center for Education Statistics, 2002.

Lawrence, J. H. "A Framework for Assessing Trends in Academic Careers." In D. Leslie (ed.), *The Growing Use of Part-Time Faculty: Understanding Causes and Effects.* New Directions for Higher Education, no. 104. San Francisco: Jossey-Bass, 1998.

Long, J. S. (ed.). *From Scarcity to Visibility: Gender Differences in the Careers of Doctoral Scientists and Engineers.* Washington, D.C.: National Academy Press, 2001.

McElrath, K. "Gender, Career Disruption, and Academic Rewards." *Journal of Higher Education*, 1992, 63(3), 269–281.

Parsad, B., and Glover, D. *Tenure Status of Postsecondary Instructional Faculty and Staff, 1992–98.* NCES 2002–210. Washington, D.C.: National Center for Education Statistics, 2002.

Perna, L. W. "The Relationship Between Family Responsibilities and Employment Status Among College and University Faculty." *Journal of Higher Education*, 2001, 72(5), 584–611.

Reagan, B. R. "Report of the Committee on the Status of Women in the Economics Profession." *American Economic Review*, 1975, 65, 490–501.

U.S. Department of Education. National Center for Education Statistics. *Digest of Education Statistics 2002*. Washington, D.C.: U.S. Government Printing Office, 2003. http://nces.ed.gov/programs/digest/d02/tables/dt246.asp.

U.S. Department of Education. National Center for Education Statistics. National Study of Postsecondary Faculty, 1999 Data Analysis System. Washington, D.C.: National Center for Education Statistics, n.d. http://www.nces.ed.gov/DAS/. Database.

Wilson, L. *The Academic Man: A Study in the Sociology of a Profession*. New York: Oxford University Press, 1942.

VALERIE MARTIN CONLEY is assistant professor of higher education and associate director of the Center for Higher Education at Ohio University.

3

Universities reported that when work/family policies were used, they often inspired loyalty and a sense of community among faculty.

Work/Family Policies in Higher Education: Survey Data and Case Studies of Policy Implementation

Carol S. Hollenshead, Beth Sullivan, Gilia C. Smith, Louise August, Susan Hamilton

Today's American families face a juggling act of home and work, school, medical care, after-school activities, and other responsibilities required to raise a family and maintain a household. Studies produced by advocates in the nonprofit sector indicate the need for improved family leave benefits and document substantial interest in the area by policymakers at the state level (Holcomb, 2001).

Since the empowerment of the employee at the organizational level and the move from standardization to flexibility is an essential part of the new postmodern and postbureaucratic organization (Kumar, 1995), employers across the country have begun to respond to this new philosophy. Increasingly employers have developed policies that acknowledge the need for a healthy balance between work and home. In fact, more than one-third of American companies now offer maternity leave in excess of that guaranteed by the Family and Medical Leave Act (FMLA), and another 15 percent offer the same leave to new fathers, adoptive parents, or employees with sick dependents (Holcomb, 2001). These policies allow employees greater flexibility in the way they use their sick time, schedule their work hours, fulfill their duties, and interweave pregnancy, childbirth, and parenting with careers. Studies in the corporate sector have demonstrated that better work/family balance ultimately leads to improvements in employee morale (Galinsky, Friedman, and Hernandez, 1991) and is increasingly viewed by managers in both the corporate and nonprofit sectors as cost effective.

NEW DIRECTIONS FOR HIGHER EDUCATION, no. 130, Summer 2005 © Wiley Periodicals, Inc.

But to what degree do institutions of higher education have such policies in place for their faculty? In 2001, the American Association of University Professors (AAUP) declared that "the development and implementation of institutional policies that enable the healthy integration of work responsibilities with family life in academe requires renewed attention." A 1996 study conducted by the Foundation of the College and University Personnel Association and the Families and Work Institute provides helpful answers to some of these questions. The *College and University Reference Guide to Work/Family Programs* offers a snapshot of the policies and programs available to faculty and staff in the mid-1990s (Friedman, Rimsky, and Johnson, 1996). This study took the important first step of surveying a broad array of policy and program options in existence at American institutions.

In recent years, a number of studies documenting and analyzing the use of work/family policies in academic institutions have examined the variety of methods institutions use to help faculty balance their responsibilities to work and to families. Policies most frequently researched include those allowing faculty to stop the tenure clock (American Association of University Professors, 2001; Wilson, 2001), work part time (Drago and Williams, 2000; Leslie and Walke, 2001), or negotiate with department chairs to modify job duties (Cramer and Boyd, 1995). Parental leave policies for child care or elder care and policies supporting dual-career couples are also frequently discussed. In addition, current research documents the institutional costs of not accommodating family caregiving and barriers to the implementation and utilization of work/family policies in academic institutions (Friedman, Rimsky, and Johnson, 1996).

Theoretical and descriptive studies link the limited availability of work/family policies to the slow improvement of women's status within the professoriate (AAUP, 2001; Drago and Williams, 2000). Although the number of women in academia continues to increase, women are disproportionately represented in non-tenure-track positions, at nondoctoral institutions, and among low salary grades (AAUP, 2001; Glazer-Raymo, 1999; Rhoads and Rhoads, 2003; Hollenshead and others, 2003). Moreover, tenured and tenure-track women are less likely to have children than tenured and tenure-track men (Mason and Goulden, 2002). Researchers concur that the model academic career path and tenure system often conflicts with a faculty member's familial responsibilities. Women continue to perform the majority of caregiving tasks in most U.S. families and are thus disproportionately affected by conflicts between the ideal academic career trajectory and family needs (Hochschild, 1989; Drago and Williams, 2000). Nevertheless, there has been increased interest in developing policies that are available to men.

The research on work/family policies in institutions of higher education is conducted by investigators from a variety of fields, including higher education, organizational theory, social work, women's studies, labor studies, family studies, and psychology. Methodologies range from quantitative national surveys to historical and theoretical contextual studies. This lack of homogeneity in research methods is matched to some extent by the divergent organizational systems and political climates of the universities being studied.

Many work/family policies are implemented in varying ways within institutions, often on a case-by-case basis, making data collection challenging. Thus, it is unclear if and how various institutions implement work/family policies or how such policies are received and used by faculty. In order to help fill this gap, we studied the policies of a cross-section of universities and examined in detail in a smaller number of institutions how those policies were developed, used, and perceived.

The Faculty Work/Family Policy Study

The Faculty Work/Family Policy Study, undertaken by the University of Michigan's Center for the Education of Women, analyzed policies and programs from a large, representative sample of U.S. institutions stratified by Carnegie classification. Funded by the Alfred P. Sloan Foundation, the study included a Web-based survey of 648 universities and colleges, of which 255 (39 percent) responded. This was followed by a telephone survey of 51 of those respondents. The study delved into questions regarding the development, administration, and use of faculty work/family policies in an attempt to address the following questions:

- Do work/family policies for faculty vary by the Carnegie classification of the institution, or are certain policies becoming the norm?
- Are policies based on written, formal policy or on informal practice?
- What are the eligibility and entitlement criteria for these policies?
- What barriers exist to the creation of family-friendly policies? What types of environments facilitate their implementation?
- To what extent are work/family policies used by faculty? If the rate of use is particularly low or high, why might that be?

The study revealed some interesting findings on these points, which are detailed later in the chapter. The work/family policies examined were tenure clock stop, modified duties, paid leave while recovering from childbirth, paid dependent care leave, unpaid dependent care leave in excess of the twelve weeks mandated by FMLA, reduced appointments for ordinary or extraordinary dependent care needs, and the availability of part-time and job-share appointments. In addition, the study probed the existence of individuals or units designated to assist faculty with work/family issues, as well as employment assistance to spouses or partners of faculty.

We recognize that a good deal of policy implementation, especially when informal practice is considered, is decided at the unit level within colleges. However, this study chose to take an institution-wide view to various aspects of policy development, administration and use.

Work/Family Policies and Programs Defined

While the meaning behind some policies or programs is self-evident by their name, other work/family initiatives are not as clearly understood. For this reason, we briefly review the meanings of key policies and programs studied.

Tenure Clock Stop. Of the policies examined, the one most commonly provided was tenure clock stop. Tenure clock stop policies allow a tenure-track faculty member to have a temporary pause in the tenure clock to accommodate special circumstances. At the end of such a pause, the clock resumes ticking with the same number of years left to tenure review as when it paused. Circumstances occasioning the use of this policy include birth or adoption of a child, serious medical illness of the faculty member, or extensive care needs by a dependent of the faculty member. This policy is also sometimes referred to as a tenure clock extension.

While most colleges that have a tenure clock stop policy make this policy available to both men and women faculty, women's greater need for this policy should be noted. Since the timing of the tenure process tends to overlap with the childbearing years, the pursuit of tenure often conflicts with a woman's decision to have children. It has been suggested that use of a pause in the tenure clock allows women faculty to adjust better to the demands of a new infant without permanently derailing their careers.

Modified Duties. Modified duties policies allow a faculty member to reduce her or his teaching, research, or service load for a temporary period (usually a term or two) without a commensurate reduction in pay. Teaching demands often make it difficult for faculty members to use traditional sick or disability leaves. Therefore, modified duties policies provide a method for responding to the needs of faculty caring for infants, elders, or critically ill spouses or partners. For women faculty who are recovering from childbirth, a modified duties policy may be seen as equivalent to the six to eight weeks of full-time paid sick leave most universities offer women in staff positions.

Paid Leave to Recover from Childbirth. Because leaves for women recovering from childbirth can fall under many different names, our survey asked how institutions provided paid time off for faculty women who are pregnant or recuperating from childbirth. It was important to separate this leave from dependent care leave, which does not involve physical recovery of the faculty member but is simply designed to allow care for another individual.

Paid Dependent Care Leave. The variety of dependent care leaves is more complex than one might expect. Examples of dependent care leave for infant care include parental leave, maternity or paternity leave, and adoptive parent leave. Many colleges that have such dependent care leaves also include care for ailing parents, spouses, or partners.

Unpaid Dependent Care Leave. The FMLA establishes that employers with fifty or more employees must allow up to twelve weeks of unpaid leave in order to care for a newly born, adopted, or fostered child; receive care for a serious health condition; or assist a family member who is receiving such care. Federal rules list a number of individuals who meet the definition of a "qualified family member." While FMLA rules do not consider parents-in-law, significant others, and domestic partners as qualified family members, employers are free to include additional categories of individuals under an expanded definition of "qualified family member" if the employer so chooses. For the purposes of this study, the term *dependent* referred to individuals such as young children; disabled adult children; elderly, ill, or disabled parents or siblings; and ill, injured, or disabled spouses or partners.

Reduced, Part-Time, and Job-Share Appointments. Reduced, part-time, or job-share appointments are defined as those in which a faculty member works less than 100 percent for the institution. For the purposes of this study, the distinction was made between part-time appointments from the date of hire and reduced appointments, in which full-time appointments were reduced to part time after the date of hire. For these appointments, pay is proportionate to the percentage of effort reflected by the appointment. Split appointments (those involving two units of the same institution) were not defined as part-time, reduced, or job-share appointments for the purposes of this study.

In the Web-based survey, we differentiated between reduced appointments for extraordinary reasons (for example, to care for an injured child, spouse, or partner) and reduced appointments for ordinary reasons (for example, to spend more time at home with young children or as a short-term transition from maternity leave).

Job-share policies allow two faculty members to each work part-time while fulfilling, between them, the requirements of one full-time faculty position.

Staff Assistance with Work/Family Policies and Employment of Spouses or Partners. One of the measures on our survey was a dichotomous variable indicating the presence (or absence) of units or personnel clearly assigned to advise faculty regarding availability and implementation of work/family balance policies. The survey also measured whether institutions provided employment assistance (such as help in job searches or job placement) for partners or spouses of faculty. These programs are sometimes referred to as dual-career hiring or trailing-spouse programs.

Methodology

The study used two instruments: an initial Web survey and a follow-up telephone survey. The process for collection of survey data began with identification of a contact person at each institution who was knowledgeable and willing to return the requested survey information. Researchers called the executive officer in charge of academic affairs and requested to speak with someone knowledgeable regarding faculty policies. This contact (usually from the office of academic affairs, human resources, or institutional research) was asked to complete and submit a short Web-based survey. A paper version was also available.

Table 3.1. Description of the Sample

	Research I and II	Doctoral I and II	Master's I and II	Baccalaureate I and II	Associate	Total
Number surveyed	123	38	180	198	109	648
Number returned	73	16	66	70	30	255
Response rate	59%	42%	35%	35%	28%	39%

The sample developed for the survey was a stratified random sample of 704 institutions from the 2000 Carnegie list (although using the 1994 classifications). The reason for using the 1994 rankings was to provide a finer breakdown by institutional rank than the 2000 ranking provides.

The sample strategy was to select approximately 35 percent of the institutions within each Carnegie category. Due to their small number, all research institutions were included in the sample. And due to their large numbers, a smaller fraction of Associate degree institutions were included in the sample. In addition, all institutions with membership in the College and University Work/Family Association were included in the sample, as were "leadership campuses" as defined in an earlier study (Friedman, Rimsky, and Johnson, 1996). With the exception of specialty schools in the area of technology, nine types of specialized institution categories (such as tribal colleges, free-standing law schools, and theological seminaries) were excluded. Technology schools were originally included in the sample because of their particular significance to the Sloan Foundation, funder of the research. Due to a low response rate from these schools, however, their results are not included in the analysis. From the original sample of 704 schools, the list of potential respondents was reduced to 648, primarily due to some institutions' refusal to provide an assigned respondent for the survey.

From the 648 survey recipients, the Center for the Education of Women received 255 responses to the first stage of the study. Response rates across the sample varied by Carnegie classification (see Table 3.1). Thirty-nine percent of the sample responded to the initial Web-based survey.

The Web Survey

There were four versions of the Web-based survey: one was for institutions without tenure or identified research faculty; another was for institutions with tenure but without research faculty; a third was for institutions with both tenure and research faculty; a fourth was for institutions without tenure but with research faculty. (It should be noted, however, that although there were schools in the original sample that fell into this final category, none responded to the survey.) The contact person for each institution chose the appropriate survey.

Table 3.2. Number of Institution-Wide Formal Policies

Number of Policies	Research I and II (n = 73)	Doctoral I and II (n = 16)	Master's I and II (n = 66)	Baccalaureate I and II (n = 70)	Associate (n = 30)	All Institutions Total (n = 255)	
0	7%	31%	38%	51%	50%	34%	86
1	18	25	30	19	37	24	61
2	22	25	14	13	7	16	42
3	21	13	12	9	0	12	34
4	7	6	0	6	3	4	16
5	8	0	3	1	3	4	27
6	18	0	2	1	0	6	10
7	0	0	2	0	0	0	7
8	0	0	0	0	0	0	10
Average number of policies[a]	2.99	1.38	1.29	1.09	0.80	1.67	

[a]Note: The differences in the average number of policies between research institutions and all other types of institutions were statistically significant at levels of p ≤ .001 or better.

For the purposes of this study, *faculty member* was defined as an individual with a regular instructional appointment or anyone with a regular faculty research appointment (a researcher who can serve as a principal investigator or coprincipal investigator on a research grant and whose primary responsibility does not involve regular teaching). This definition did not include lecturers, clinical faculty, visiting, or adjunct faculty. The term *dependent* referred to individuals such as young children; disabled adult children; elderly, ill, or disabled parents or siblings; and ill, injured, or disabled spouses or partners.

The next several sections summarize the results of the Web survey.

Average Number of Policies Offered. Based on the survey responses, we tallied the number of work/family policies each institution had that were institution-wide and formal. On average, institutions reported having fewer than two institution-wide policies. However, research institutions reported twice as many policies as other schools in the sample. (See Table 3.2.)

We also looked separately at elite baccalaureate institutions—those named to the *U.S. News and World Report* list of top one hundred liberal arts colleges in the country. When we analyzed the number of policies held by institutions considered elite versus the remaining baccalaureate colleges among our respondents, we found the elite baccalaureates had 2.53 policies on average, while other baccalaureates had 0.69 policies. We surmise that elite baccalaureate colleges, in competition for faculty with research institutions, have developed a greater number of family-friendly policies as a recruitment strategy.

Policies Less Available to Research Faculty. The study sought to answer whether research faculty were eligible to use work/family policies to the same extent as tenure-track or tenured faculty. For every policy on

Table 3.3. Formal and Informal Institution-Wide Policies by Institution Type

	Research I and II (n = 73)	Doctoral I and II (n = 16)	Master's I and II (n = 66)	Baccalaureate I and II (n = 70)	Associate (n = 30)	Total (n = 255)
Tenure clock stop						
Formal	86%	44%	32%	23%	7%	43%
Informal	4	13	6	9	0	6
No policy	10	43	62	68	93	51
Modified duties						
Formal	32	13	12	17	3	18
Informal	6	0	3	19	7	8
No policy	62	87	85	64	90	74
Paid dependent care						
Formal	22	6	15	16	7	16
Informal	1	0	2	9	3	4
No policy	77	94	83	75	90	80
Unpaid leave beyond FMLA						
Formal	53	44	39	24	43	40
Informal	12	6	15	9	10	11
No policy	35	50	46	67	47	49
Reduced appointment, extraordinary needs						
Formal	29	19	9	7	7	15
Informal	0	0	0	0	0	0
No policy	71	81	91	93	93	85
Reduced appointment, ordinary needs						
Formal	29	6	9	6	7	13
Informal	12	13	15	17	17	15
No policy	59	81	76	77	76	72
Part time/job share						
Formal	23	6	9	13	7	14
Informal	0	0	0	0	0	0
No policy	77	94	91	87	93	86
Employment assistance						
Formal	25	0	3	3	0	9
Informal	43	19	14	16	10	22
No policy	32	81	83	81	90	69

the survey, we found that research faculty were one-third to one-half as likely as their colleagues to be eligible to use these policies.

Formal versus Informal Policy. Respondents were asked to specify whether institution-wide policies were formal and written or informal and based on individual arrangements. (See Table 3.3.) Not surprisingly, we discovered that the research institutions, which are often more complex and have greater resources, were more likely than other Carnegie types to have formalized policies.

Our survey did not ask about the formal or informal nature of policies providing paid time off for recovery from childbirth. This is because the Pregnancy Discrimination Act of 1978 requires institutions to provide paid time off for pregnancy and childbirth if they provide paid time off for other forms of illness or disability. Given this requirement, we assumed the majority of paid leave policies for recovery following pregnancy would be formal.

Dependents for Whom Work/Family Policies Can Be Used. We sought to determine whether institutions made their work/family policies available to faculty to different degrees, based on the type of dependent needing care. We also questioned whether institutions attempt to be gender blind in their application of policy for faculty with dependent care needs. For each policy relating to dependent care needs, we asked, "For what types of dependents may a faculty member take X policy?" Respondents could choose any or all of the following answer choices:

- A woman faculty member may use the policy if she is pregnant or gives birth to a child.
- A man or woman faculty member may use the policy if a child is born into the household.
- A man or woman faculty member may use the policy if a child is adopted or fostered into the household.
- A man or woman faculty member may use the policy to care for an adult or child who is ill, injured, or disabled.

Results on this measure of eligibility are detailed below.

Tenure Clock Stop. Of all the policies examined in this study, the one provided most often was tenure clock stop. When analyzed in terms of the types of dependents for whom a faculty member could request a tenure stop, we found that master's and baccalaureate institutions were less likely to make this policy available to male faculty who had a child born into the household than they were to a woman faculty member who gave birth. Research, doctoral, and Associate degree institutions, however, took a more gender-blind approach to this policy by offering it to both women and men equally.

It should be noted that cost was the barrier most often cited by institutions to the implementation of work/family leave policy in Friedman, Rimsky, and Johnson's 1996 study. But while tenure clock stop might bear an opportunity cost for the individual, it bears no direct cost for the institution. As might be expected, tenure clock stop policies have the strongest showing at institutions where research and original scholarship are core institutional missions and are critical to tenure achievement.

Modified Duties Leave. Overall, 18 percent of institutions carried a formal modified duties policy, although it is noteworthy that percentages were closer to one-third for the research institutions and zero for the

Associate degree colleges. Modified duties policies were more likely to be provided to women faculty who give birth than for other dependent care reasons.

Unpaid Dependent Care Leave in Excess of FMLA. Not surprisingly, universities offer their faculty unpaid leaves to a much greater extent than paid leaves. Forty percent of the sample reported having a formal institution-wide policy offering more than the twelve weeks of unpaid dependent care leave required under FMLA. Research institutions were somewhat more likely to have unpaid dependent care leave beyond FMLA than were other types of institutions.

Respondents were asked to indicate the maximum number of days or weeks offered by their policies (beyond FMLA), whether the amount of leave was negotiable, or whether it would be determined in some other fashion. Sixty percent of respondents indicated the amount of leave was negotiable, 23 percent provided "other" responses, and 17 percent indicated a specific number of days or weeks. Among this 17 percent, the maximum number of days offered beyond FMLA was fairly evenly distributed across a range of between 1 and 364 days.

Paid Dependent Care Leave. Sixteen percent of respondents reported having formal institution-wide policies for paid dependent care leave. Institutions tended to offer this policy to both women and men faculty with newborns more often than to women childbearers exclusively.

While unpaid dependent care leave in excess of FMLA is an important barometer of where institutions stand with respect to federal standards, the literature (Han and Waldfogel, 2003) and common sense indicate that paid leaves have much greater impact on employees' lives. Given the cost of paid leaves at the institutional level, it is not surprising that they are found less frequently than are unpaid dependent care leaves. Our findings corroborate the assertion that "institutions with larger budgets and larger student bodies are more likely to offer family-friendly programs and policies" (Friedman, Rimsky, and Johnson, 1996, p. 2).

Reduced, Part-Time, and Job-Share Appointments. Only 14 percent of the sample reported having formal, institution-wide policies that gave employees access to reduced appointments for extraordinary reasons such as the severe illness of a dependent. In the case of reduced appointments for ordinary reasons, such as a desire to spend more time at home with a young child, 13 percent of the sample reported the existence of formal, institution-wide policies. In the case of appointments that were offered as part-time or job share, 14 percent of the sample reported the existence of formal, institution-wide policies supporting such positions. For all three policies, research institutions were the most likely of all Carnegie types to offer these options.

We found it noteworthy that 15 percent of institutions had an informal, institution-wide policy of allowing reduced appointments in response to ordinary needs. For extraordinary reasons, however, there were no institutions

Table 3.4. Methods of Providing Paid Childbirth-Related Time Off by Institution Type

Policy	Research I and II (n = 73)	Doctoral I and II (n = 16)	Master's I and II (n = 66)	Baccalaureate I and II (n = 70)	Associate (n = 30)	Total (n = 255)
Sick leave	77%	56%	79%	47%	90%	69%
Disability leave	51	50	44	37	33	43
Vacation leave	51	31	36	17	43	36
Maternity leave (distinct from sick, vacation, or disability)	34	6	17	34	10	25
Temporary relief from teaching, modified duties	55	44	26	49	17	40
Other	36	13	21	11	13	21

Note: Respondents could choose more than one method. Therefore, percentages total more than 100.

that had informal, institution-wide policies. With the exception of employment assistance for spouses or partners, reduced appointments were more likely than any other policy to be offered through informal mechanisms.

Employment Assistance for Spouses or Partners of Faculty. Fewer than 10 percent of the sample reported the existence of formal employment assistance programs for faculty spouses or partners; however, 22 percent indicated that such assistance was available on an informal basis. Formal dual-career programs were almost exclusively found within research institutions; one-fourth reported having them.

Methods of Providing Paid Leave Following Childbirth. Nearly 70 percent of schools reported providing childbirth-related leave in the form of sick leave. The second most common method was disability leave (43 percent), followed by 36 percent offering vacation leave. On average, only a quarter of the schools in the sample provided women with a paid maternity leave. Although survey language for the fourth category was "temporary relief from teaching or other modification of a faculty member's duties for one term or longer," data from the telephone survey lead us to believe that respondents may have chosen this response even if relief was given for less than one term in length. For example, respondents may have chosen this method of leave to reflect coverage of some of a faculty member's class sessions by colleagues. (See Table 3.4.)

Among colleges selecting "other" as one method of providing paid childbirth-related benefits, 20 percent wrote in unpaid leaves such as FMLA, displaying a lack of understanding of the paid leave definition used in the question. Alternative policies colleges described for their "other" responses were parental, personal, or family leaves; medical leaves; banking of courses by the faculty member in advance of her or his need for time off; and colleague coverage of the faculty member's classes. About 10 percent of "other" responses explained how the institution's disability coverage applied to pregnancy.

Faculty Unions. Overall, instructional faculty were more likely to be unionized than research faculty. Twenty-two percent of our Web survey respondents had unionized instructional faculty, with 7 percent of those also having unionized research faculty. None of our respondents had unionized research faculty without also having unionized instructional faculty. Of our fifty-one telephone survey respondents, fourteen (27 percent) had unionized instructional faculty. Five of the fourteen also had unionized research faculty.

The existence of a faculty union correlated with an increased chance of having certain types of formal policies among research and master's institutions. Our Web survey found that unionized master's institutions were more likely than nonunionized master's institutions to have formal policies for tenure clock stops, modified duties, and unpaid leave in excess of the twelve weeks required by FMLA. Unionized research universities were more likely than their nonunionized peers to have these policies, as well as formal policies for reduced or part-time appointments and job-sharing arrangements from the date of hire.

The Telephone Interview

We conducted telephone interviews with a subset of Web survey respondents in order to measure faculty members' use of policies, the conditions or limits applied to their use, and the factors that encouraged or discouraged policy development and use. During the interview, we asked respondents, most of them provosts or associate provosts, questions such as:

- To what extent are work/family policies used by faculty? If the rate of use is particularly low or high, why might that be?
- What types of environments and actors have facilitated the development and implementation of work/family policies?
- What barriers exist to the creation of new family-friendly policies?

We found that the one-to-one conversation of the telephone survey allowed us to gather a rich sense of the ways policies are enacted and perceived, thus complementing the purely institutional data gathered from the Web-based survey. With the telephone data, our study is able to provide the kind of strategic guidance that university administrators need as they work to develop a healthy work-life environment for new and existing faculty within their institutions.

The telephone survey participants represented the following institutional types (using the 1994 Carnegie classification): Research I or II, twenty-six (51 percent); Doctoral I or II, three (6 percent); Master's, eleven (22 percent); Baccalaureate, eight (16 percent); and Associate, three (6 percent).

In our telephone interview, we asked a variety of questions to achieve a sense of policy use by faculty. Administrators were asked two questions specific to women faculty: "What policy or policies is a pregnant faculty member most likely to use for pregnancy and childbirth?" and which "policy or policies women faculty typically use for dependent care needs, after they have recovered from childbirth" but wish to stay home longer with a newborn.

We also asked administrators to estimate how frequently their male or female faculty used any of the family-friendly policies available to them. Respondents were asked to consider only those individuals who would have been eligible to use a policy (for whatever reason) and had the need to do so within the previous year. Estimated use was gauged on a five-point scale from faculty "never" use the policy to faculty "always" use the policy when needed. Interviewers asked only about policies that were formal and offered institution-wide by the respondent's university. We recognize the limitations of administrator-reported utilization estimates.

Use of Sick Time and Disability Leave Following Childbirth. Sick time for pregnancy and childbirth was the only policy for which respondents reported high levels of policy use ("frequent" or "always"). What we learned in our telephone discussions regarding use of sick and disability leaves was quite revealing. Essentially, many institutions think one way about the policies available for recovery from childbirth, but the specific eligibility requirements of those policies may make women childbearers ineligible to use them.

First, although 69 percent of Web respondents said faculty women were able to use sick leave for recovery from childbirth, many of these respondents refuted their Web answers during the telephone interview, saying that only twelve-month faculty were eligible for traditional sick leave. The majority of faculty at these institutions were nine- or ten-month employees.

Second, 43 percent of all Web respondents said women could use disability leave while recovering from childbirth. In the telephone interviews, however, several respondents noted that disability benefits did not begin until the faculty member had been disabled for six or more weeks. Effectively, then, these institutions' paid disability leaves are not available to the majority of women faculty whose medical recovery is completed within six to eight weeks.

While some universities may claim to be compliant with the Pregnancy Discrimination Act within the letter of the law, these data highlight the problem of having practical means by which women faculty can take leave for recovery from childbirth on equal terms with their male counterparts who are recovering from other short-term medical conditions. Even at institutions where a nine-month faculty member does have sick leave benefits and may begin using disability leave as needed before or after childbirth, departments may not address coverage of women faculty's teaching responsibilities in the same manner they would for male faculty needing leave for other medical conditions.

Another important issue revealed by our survey was the impact on women retirees' pension and health care benefits. Some institutions expect women faculty to use sick leave while recovering from childbirth. But where faculty are covered by a state benefits system, women are negatively affected if that system rewards unused sick leave days by counting them toward increased pension payouts or reduced retiree health care premium charges.

Unpaid Dependent Care Leave. Only seventeen of thirty-nine respondents to the question said that women commonly used unpaid dependent care leave during their recovery time following childbirth. For women wishing to stay home with a newborn past the time of their own recovery, twenty-one of thirty-eight respondents said women typically relied on unpaid leave. When considered outside the context of childbirth, estimates of the use of unpaid dependent care leave were low, with the vast majority of institutions reporting that faculty "rarely" or only "sometimes" used this policy.

Paid Dependent Care Leave. At the few institutions where paid dependent care leave was offered, this policy generally was said to be used "frequently." Given this policy's focus on dependent care, however, it is not surprising that this policy was reported as not commonly used during women faculty members' recovery from childbirth.

Modified Duties and Tenure Clock Stop. The estimated use by men and women faculty members of both the modified duties and tenure clock stop policies ranged fairly evenly across the spectrum from "never" to "always." This was despite respondents' ranking the modified duties policy as the third most commonly used by women recovering from childbirth and by women wishing to spend more time with their child following their own recovery from childbirth. Tenure clock stop was a policy rarely mentioned as helpful to women recovering from childbirth, but was noted as the fourth most commonly used policy for those staying home with an infant following their own recovery.

Reduced Appointments. All three questions under discussion relating to use indicated that faculty request reduced appointments only "sometimes" and "rarely" in the case of covering time home to recover from childbirth or to be with a new baby after recovery. Reduced appointments were spoken of as more appealing to senior faculty wishing to negotiate a phased retirement.

The Pros and Cons of Gender-Neutral Policies

The tendency of higher education institutions to enact gender-neutral policy is clearly demonstrated by the low percentage of institutions offering paid maternity leaves as opposed to paid sick or disability leaves. This may be because institutions do not want to be perceived as offering women anything more than a medical benefit to cover those weeks when the woman is recovering from childbirth. Some respondents to our telephone interview suggested that having policies constructed to respond to multiple needs (such as personal leave that can be taken for professional, personal, medical, or family needs) made the use of such policies more acceptable to their faculty peers.

Findings from a recent study at the University of Virginia indicate, however, that women, on average, assume more child care and housekeeping activities than their spouses, even when that (male) spouse is in the midst of a dependent care leave (Rhoads and Rhoads, 2003). This raises the question of whether men are more likely than women to use dependent care leaves to accomplish professional rather than family tasks. The implication of this finding is that gender-neutral policies are not necessarily helping women to achieve a level playing field in the academy. If the same leaves women use to recover physically from childbirth, nurse a baby, and contend with lack of sleep can be used by male faculty who have wives at home to care for their newborn child while they work on their research, then these women faculty will fall behind their male peers in terms of productivity.

Some institutions have attempted to protect against such policy abuses by restricting eligibility to faculty with high levels of caregiving responsibilities. Among our fifty-one telephone survey respondents, one-quarter had language in their policies related to dependent care that required the faculty member to be the primary caregiver or a coequal caregiver or to have substantial care responsibilities for the dependent. Twelve percent specifically required the faculty member to provide a statement attesting to this fact.

After discussing policy use with administrators, we asked why they thought faculty did not take advantage of policies more often. Of the thirty-six institutions that answered this question, twelve cited fear of career repercussions as the reason for infrequent policy use. Eleven of the thirty-six said faculty were unable to afford to take unpaid time away from work. Ten institutions suggested that faculty tended not to use these policies because families were able to time the birth of their children to occur over academic breaks or otherwise accommodate family needs through the creative juggling of classes or with support from stay-at-home partners. Nine of the thirty-six respondents said faculty were too committed to their work to take leave, and six said unclear processes hampered faculty's use of policies. These findings suggest areas where universities can focus their attention in order to increase faculty use of family-friendly policies.

Strategies for Successful Policy Development and Use

A director of academic personnel described his institution's support of work/family policies as deriving from "a consciousness that we needed to be—it was in the university's best interest to be—open to these things." So what do universities do in order to develop, implement, and improve the use of their work/family policies for faculty? Our interviews revealed five key strategies:

- Use data to promote a work/family balance agenda.
- Foster collaboration between individual policy champions and institutional committees to ensure successful policy development.
- Formalize policies and make them entitlements.
- Educate faculty and administrators about the policies on a continuous basis.
- Address climate issues that discourage faculty from using work/family policies.

Data. Universities found policy development was much more easily accomplished when data from surveys or other research on the work/family environment were available to bolster their proposals. Seventeen of our fifty-one telephone interview respondents reported their institutions had conducted research on work/family climate for faculty. This research most often took the form of climate surveys; some focused on faculty issues alone, and others addressed both faculty and staff topics. Other research included reviews of institutional data on policy use, exit interviews, policy comparisons with peer institutions, and comparisons of the tenure achievement rates of faculty who stopped the tenure clock versus those who did not.

One institution's story exemplifies the snowball effect that data gathering can inspire. In the early 1990s, a work/family task force of staff and faculty led to creation of a position and a survey. The task force and survey was sponsored by a senior vice president, a male, who was very concerned about these issues. The survey led to other discussions and initiatives. The position spun off from the associate vice president for human relations office into a new human relations office: Workforce Diversity, Equity, and Life Quality.

As we discuss in the following section, champions of work/family issues are often the ones to commission or request such climate surveys in order to raise awareness of faculty needs and elevate the discussion toward potential solutions.

Measurement is also a tool administrators can and should use to guide an institution's progress on work/family objectives. One helpful measure is tracking whether use of the tenure clock stop affects faculty members' tenure achievement. While shockingly few of the institutions in our telephone survey collected these data (only three of fifty-one), many said such information was needed to help address fears among some faculty that using this policy might harm their chances for tenure. Regular comparisons between the tenure achievement rate of policy users and nonusers are fairly simple. These analyses can also be done to discern any differences in tenure achievement by race or gender. Universities typically look at a cohort of assistant professors hired eight or nine years prior and define the current

status of each faculty member within the cohort within one of four categories: left the university without achieving tenure, achieved tenure, still pending tenure review, or at the university in a non-tenure-track position. We acknowledge that the first category will combine faculty who were denied tenure with those who leave prior to tenure review but may have been expected to achieve tenure. Nevertheless, this is a reasonable measure, as well as one that is achievable under most data systems and one we suggest be done regularly. Some institutions choose to conduct exit interviews of departing faculty in order to clarify the reasons faculty have for leaving prior to tenure review.

Another measure that was seen as valuable, but infrequently done due to the lack of formalized metrics, was feedback on the family friendliness of chairs and deans as part of their annual evaluations. Many institutions said that openness by administrators to their faculty members' use of work/family policies was considered during evaluations, but only in informal ways. More formal means of assessing the work/family climate in a department or school would better hold chairs and deans accountable for the pivotal role they play in shaping the culture within their span of control.

Policy Champions. More than half of our fifty-one telephone interview respondents named their president and provost as actors instrumental in the development of work/family policies for faculty. More than one-third said that deans, committees on the status of women, and faculty senate committees that addressed benefits, diversity, or recruitment and retention played a key role in policy development. Again, more than one-third said that individual faculty members played important roles in spearheading successful policy development on their campuses. As would be expected, human resource offices were described as instrumental in the process of developing work/family policies by two-thirds of the institutions. One-quarter of those surveyed indicated their faculty union was influential in policy development.

We found that the effect of women's involvement in policies extended beyond university committees on the status of women. Twenty-four percent of respondents indicated that women's centers, women's studies programs, and other women's organizations were instrumental in shaping their college's policy deliberations. One respondent described instances in which an individual or committee raised the need for new family-friendly policies as "the process of addressing the squeaky wheel."

Although 84 percent of our telephone survey respondents had units or individuals assigned to help faculty on work/family issues, these work-life resources were not reported to be key contributors to policy development. There was, however, a clear and positive correlation between the degree to which an institution had a variety of formalized policies and the likelihood that it had dedicated work/family resources. We surmise that the existence of such resources is an indicator of an institution's progress toward achieving a comprehensive array of family-friendly policies and services.

When asked, "What type of development or advocacy efforts led to establishment of work/family policies at your institution?" nearly one-third of those interviewed (sixteen of fifty-one) described a push to ameliorate the tension between parenting and work for faculty women. Thirteen of fifty-one mentioned concerns regarding equitable treatment for women, lesbian or gay faculty, or faculty of color as inspiring action on their campuses. Seven respondents said discussions regarding access and financial support for child care were triggers for advocacy within their institutions. Occasionally work/family policy achievements were accomplished in response to external pressures such as accreditation reviews or lawsuits. In a few cases, discussion regarding the provision of health insurance benefits to domestic partners spurred reflection on the eligibility of gay or lesbian faculty to use work/family policies to care for their domestic partner or the children of their partner.

Formalize Policies and Make Them Entitlements. Many institutions found that formalizing policy simply acknowledged what was already current practice in their schools or departments. Policy formalization raised the visibility of the policy so that both faculty and administrators had a clearer understanding of the rules for policy use. We found that reduced appointments, modified duties, and unpaid leaves were the policies most likely to be informally negotiated.

Having a formal policy on the books increased goodwill among existing faculty and was seen as a recruitment tool for attracting new faculty. It also improved the climate for faculty by acknowledging that most faculty will have a family need to manage at some point during their career, whether for young children, a dying parent, or an ill spouse or partner.

Many colleges found they benefited from outlining the circumstances under which faculty were entitled to use each policy. This relieved individual administrators from having to spend time making highly personal, case-by-case decisions each time a faculty member requested use of a policy. Among the twenty respondents with a formal institution-wide policy providing paid dependent care leave, twelve made this type of leave an entitlement. Among the twelve institutions with a formal institution-wide policy allowing modified duties, four made it an entitlement. Formal policies regarding unpaid dependent care leave in excess of FMLA and reduced appointments were not as likely as other policies to be structured as entitlements.

Of the thirty-nine institutions with a formal institution-wide tenure clock stop policy, fifteen had specific criteria for entitlements. Nine of these fifteen institutions making it an entitlement did so for reasons specific to childbirth, adoption or fostering of a child, or newborn care by a primary caregiver. The other six of these fifteen institutions entitled both male and female faculty to use the tenure clock stop for a broader array of reasons. Of the nine institutions that limited entitlement to women faculty or new children in the home, five had additional policy provisions that made fathers of newborns or faculty caring for other types of dependents eligible to request tenure stop, with use granted at the discretion of the administration.

One theme that emerged from our analysis was that the nature of informal leaves and the process of negotiation that they necessitate makes exercise of such policies much less frequent than formalized policies. When institutions formalize policies and entitlement reasons, as one administrator put it, faculty "know the benefits are entitlements and there's no stigma attached" to using them.

Educate Faculty and Administration About the Policies. Institutions need to make sure that information about policies is thoroughly disseminated to all relevant constituencies. Universities used new faculty orientations, information sessions for deans and chairs, their faculty handbooks, and Web sites as their main methods for policy education. Some institutions also use existing faculty and administrative forums to remind audiences of family-friendly policies and address perceptions about their costs and benefits. Brochures and programs on work/family balance are other avenues colleges use to promote the availability of policies for faculty.

Frequent sharing of policy information is critical for many reasons, including the regular turnover among department chairs and the addition of new faculty. Furthermore, not all faculty members will need information about family-friendly policies at orientation, yet many may require it later when they are expecting a child or are presented with an elder care crisis. Periodic communication of work/family information allows faculty members and administrators to be aware of the latest university offerings. Faculty are more likely to use policies that are well advertised and less likely to be resentful of administrators if they need to use a family-friendly policy but fail to request it because they were unaware of its existence.

Address Climate Issues. Many of those responding to our telephone survey reported that a "chilly climate" sometimes discourages faculty from taking advantage of work/family policies. Twelve of thirty-six respondents cited faculty members' fear of possible career repercussions as the reason work/family policies were not used as often as they might be. Other respondents raised climate concerns in the context of answering other questions during the interview. We believe that every institution needs to address climate issues, whether that institution is seeking to develop its first work/family policies or to create an environment in which faculty feel safe using existing ones.

Some administrators referenced "workaholic" cultures in certain departments or schools where a colleague's family leave might be characterized as showing a lack of professionalism or a willingness to shift burdens onto one's colleagues. In such environments, faculty were said to feel pressure to come back and cover their classes. One respondent noted that "untenured faculty say 'I'm afraid how my colleagues will react to my taking leave.' Even the notion of getting pregnant makes many fear not getting tenure." The respondent described this as a "cultural belief," held by both men and women, that taking leave is "inappropriate behavior" and thus likely to affect the tenure outcome. A male human resource director at another institution used these terms to describe reactions in a particular school to faculty taking family leave: "Treatment doesn't vary in terms of official responses that rise to the HR level. But there is a subtle variance or pressure at the department or dean's level. 'You are not here, and everybody else is.'"

Many we interviewed noted that use of these policies was not well received in traditionally male-dominated departments, such as engineering, business, and the sciences. "Women are watched more in terms of how they fit in," commented one respondent from a research university. Another noted, "It has to do with the discipline and the respect for women in those disciplines. Where there's a critical mass [of women], there's more likely to be a difference." A male assistant provost from another research university described climate issues this way:

> The cultures and traditions in the departments, as well as the balance of faculty (percent male to female), will affect [policy] usage. Historically male departments affect informal word of mouth and things you should pay attention to. The role of chair is very important. If very supportive of policies, you will see more use of the policies. If in a rotating position, or not willing, you could see a different result. You hear apocryphal tales that so-and-so didn't use leave because a senior male in her department would frown on it. This does occur in some cases.

However, such beliefs were no longer described as monolithic, but remain in isolated areas of the university. One of our telephone survey respondents cogently described the changing perceptions within academia about women's professional roles and men's parenting roles: "As more women move into faculty ranks, family issues come to the fore and we respond to them. Also, male expectations about coparenting are incredibly different from twenty years ago. Society influences demand [for work/ family policies]."

Leaders within higher education are increasingly called on to manage the impact of this cultural change as it affects their institutions. Management of these different cultural views also requires sensitivity to competing views by age cohorts. We learned that some senior women faculty, having struggled to survive in academia without a supportive work/family environment, sometimes project the same "pull yourself up by your bootstraps" attitudes as their male peers. Having succeeded in their own professional life, sometimes by forgoing a spouse or partner or children to do so, they are resistant to work/family accommodations suggested for junior faculty. Nevertheless, one preeminent research university noted having managers who want to use their institutional position as a source of culture change: "We are particularly concerned about the culture at the graduate level. This is the point where people formulate their understanding of what sacrifices are made [to succeed in academia]." This attention to culture as it affects the future pipeline of faculty is one example of what makes this institution a leader among research universities.

At universities where an institutional champion advocated for improved balance between work and family responsibilities, respondents characterized the environment as genuinely responsive to professional and personal needs. When positive statements about work/family balance are made by the president or provost or voiced in departmental, dean, or faculty meetings, this can shape an institution's culture to be more accepting of all faculty members' needs. Chairs and deans play an important role in shaping attitudes about the academic value of faculty with family responsibilities when they make it clear to tenure and promotion committees that faculty must not be penalized for using university policies. Indeed, it is clear that individual leadership makes a difference.

Self-interest and the bottom line were mentioned by respondents as part of the reason their leadership was instituting family-friendly policies for faculty. Universities reported that when work/family policies were used, they often inspired loyalty and a sense of community among faculty. As an associate provost at one research university told us, "It's not just altruism. We do things to keep our faculty." Another research university's associate provost pointed to work/family policies and their impact on retention when she noted that some junior women faculty are prepared to say, "I'm not going to be at an institution if they're going to hold it against me for stopping the tenure clock."

Those surveyed indicated that good feelings not only go a long way toward improving retention rates, but are also evident to prospective faculty who come for recruitment visits. Quite often, the demand to recruit new faculty drove creation of work/family policies, and therefore the cost to offer the policies has been considered part of an institution's recruitment expenditures. More and more, competition for talented young faculty is driving universities to improve their portfolio of family-friendly policies and programs.

Gay and Lesbian Faculty. From our interviews, it is clear that the design of work/family policies applicable to gay and lesbian faculty is the next frontier for many colleges and universities. When asked what policy development efforts were currently under way at their institutions, nearly one-quarter of those responding (eight of thirty-four) mentioned domestic partner insurance benefits or clarifications in policy regarding the eligibility of gay and lesbian faculty. In some cases, policy revisions were due to changes in state law; other cases were driven by changes in university health insurance coverage.

It is important to note that language clearly making gay and lesbian faculty eligible to use work/family policies to care for their domestic partners is still the exception, not the rule. We were surprised to find that institutions considered heterosexual partners within their definitions of "domestic partners" almost as frequently as they included same-sex partners. A number of those surveyed mentioned using purposely vague language, such as "persons residing within your household," in order to be able to interpret their policies as applicable to gays and lesbians without antagonizing constituencies who oppose gay rights.

Other Current Initiatives. Other initiatives under development at respondent institutions included campus-based child care programs, spousal hiring programs, and efforts related to tenure. Specific tenure initiatives involved creation of a phased retirement program that would allow senior faculty to retain their tenure status, allowance for a tenure clock stop while faculty work part time, a review of the tenure evaluation process, and an examination of the feasibility of having part-time tenure-track positions.

Opposition to Work/Family Policies

When respondents were asked where resistance to work/family policy came from, their answers often varied depending on which policy was being considered. Six respondents reported that faculty, unions, or executive officers had concerns about who was able to benefit from the proposed policy and who was not. The type of policy most often debated in these contexts was maternity or paternity leave. While one respondent couched this resistance in terms of "equity," the rest of these responses disaggregated quite clearly along gender lines. For example, resistance to maternity or paternity leaves was said to emerge "from subcultures in the university that are male-dominated and senior in age and experience. This impacts informally in terms of expectations in departments and in governance committee deliberations in which they argue for fair treatment (e.g., single individual versus family for insurance premiums)."

A related but more passive form of resistance was evidenced by reluctance to institutionalize work/family policy. The argument for case-by-case application (observed in the example above and in other cases) was usually articulated in conjunction with the perception that work/family policies were of benefit only to women.

Domestic partnership benefits were the policy most often cited as the site of resistance to work/family policy. Six institutions specifically mentioned difficulty getting approval for domestic partnership benefits from their boards of trustees or regents. In several cases, it was noted that the state legislature pressured the board not to ratify these policies. In one instance, action was being taken against the board by the state legislature as a retaliatory measure for approval of domestic partnership benefits.

Funding constraints were often cited as the source of generalized resistance to work/family policy. This view was reinforced by other information we received from our Web survey respondents, many of whom were considering new or expanded policies at the time of the survey. When contacted within a year for the telephone interview, most said that budget cutbacks had forestalled any new developments. During the telephone interview regarding opposition to work/family policies, two respondents from public institutions mentioned a zero-sum budget mentality at their institutions, where any discussion of new programs was framed in the context of having to take away from existing programs.

In one case, however, the respondent felt that the institution's focus on budget was simply used as an excuse for inaction. This view is supported by information from another question in the telephone survey, in which respondents were asked if additional money was available to help departments cover the replacement costs for the teaching or other duties of a faculty member on leave. Forty-nine percent of respondents (twenty-five of fifty-one) said additional funding was available to assist departments, often coming from the provost or from some other central budget.

Recommendations for Further Study

Our study broached the surface of several topics worthy of research in greater depth. In particular, we would like to understand the reasons that elite baccalaureate institutions have nearly as many family-friendly policies as research universities, surpassing all other Carnegie types. Such a study could address our hypothesis that competition with research universities for quality faculty is a major driver for policy development by the elite baccalaureate institutions.

Another area deserving of further study is whether faculty who use work/family policies are any less likely to achieve tenure than faculty who do not use them. Cohort analyses of faculty tenure achievement are relatively simple to conduct. Especially if combined with exit interviews, a tenure achievement study done at a number of institutions would provide clear data to either affirm or allay faculty fears about the potential career repercussions of policy use.

In a similar vein, we recommend studies of the impact on tenure achievement of reduced faculty appointments. Anecdotal evidence suggests that women sometimes move from tenure-track to non-tenure-track positions in order to balance their academic career with the needs of young children. It is unclear whether this movement is often required by university policy or climate or made by choice. Our study demonstrated that colleges do not yet have formal policies that allow reduced appointments for such ordinary dependent care reasons. It would be illustrative to know the degree to which institutional policies mandate movement off the tenure track for regular faculty who are not near the age of retirement but wish to hold part-time appointments.

References

American Association of University Professors. "Statement of Principles on Family Responsibilities and Academic Work." 2001. www.aaup.org/statements/reports/re01fam.htm.

Cramer, E., and Boyd, J. "The Tenure Track and the Parent Track: A Road Guide." *Wilson Library Bulletin,* 1995, *65,* 41–42.

Drago, R., and Williams, J. "A Half-Time Tenure Track Proposal." *Change,* 2000, *32*(6), 46–51.

Friedman, D. E., Rimsky, C., and Johnson, A. A. *College and University Reference Guide to Work/Family Programs.* New York: Families and Work Institute, 1996.

Galinsky, E., Friedman, D., and Hernandez, C. *The Corporate Reference Guide to Work-Family Programs.* New York: Families and Work Institute, 1991.

Glazer-Raymo, J. *Shattering the Myths: Women in Academe.* Baltimore, Md.: Johns Hopkins University Press, 1999.

Han, W. J., and Waldfogel, J. "Parental Leave: The Impact of Recent Legislation on Parents' Leave Taking." *Demography,* 2003, *40*(1), 191–200.

Hochschild, A. *The Second Shift: Working Parents and the Revolution at Home.* New York: Viking, 1989.

Holcomb, V. *Why Americans Need Family Leave Benefits.* Washington, D.C.: National Partnership for Women and Families, 2001.

Hollenshead, C., and others. *Women at the University of Michigan: A Statistical Report on the Status of Women Students, Staff and Faculty on the Ann Arbor Campus.* (4th ed.) Ann Arbor: University of Michigan, President's Advisory Commission on Women's Issues, 2003.

Kumar, K. "Cultural Diversity's Impact on Group Process and Performance." In C.J.G. Gersick (ed.), *Group Management: Current Issues in Practice and Research.* Brookfield, Vt.: Dartmouth, 1995.

Leslie, D. W., and Walke, J. "Out of the Ordinary: The Anomalous Academic." 2001. http://www.wm.edu/edu/education/Faculty/Leslie/anomacad.html.

Mason, M. A., and Goulden, M. "Do Babies Matter? The Effect of Family Formation on the Lifelong Careers of Academic Men and Women." *Academe,* 2002, *6,* 21–27.

Rhoads, S., and Rhoads, C. "Gender Roles and Gender-Neutral Post-Birth Policies." Paper presented at the American Association for Higher Education, Washington, D.C., Mar. 16, 2003.

Wilson, R. "A Push to Help New Parents Prepare for Tenure Reviews." *Chronicle of Higher Education,* Nov. 9, 2001, p. A10.

CAROL S. HOLLENSHEAD is director of the Center for the Education of Women and chair of the President's Advisory Commission on Women's Issues, both at the University of Michigan.

BETH SULLIVAN is program manager for policy and advocacy at the Center for the Education of Women, University of Michigan.

GILIA C. SMITH is a graduate researcher at the Center for the Education of Women, University of Michigan.

LOUISE AUGUST is a graduate researcher at the Center for the Education of Women, University of Michigan.

SUSAN HAMILTON is a graduate researcher at the Center for the Education of Women, University of Michigan.

4

Having a child creates priorities, adds perspective, and helps women to be clear about what they can do (and what they are willing to do) to succeed as a faculty member.

Work and Family Perspectives from Research University Faculty

Kelly Ward, Lisa E. Wolf-Wendel

Given changes in the academic workforce, including the presence of a growing number of women faculty of childbearing age, it is becoming increasingly important for institutions of higher education to consider how they react to and accommodate faculty with familial demands. Such accommodations were considered unnecessary when a majority of academic professionals were men with stay-at-home wives (Tierney and Bensimon, 1996; Williams, 2000) and when the academic labor market was such that there were too few positions for the large number of qualified applicants. Neither is the case today; the labor market is shifting, and an increasing number of academics find themselves trying to juggle academic work and parenthood (Finkelstein, Seal, and Schuster, 1998; Perna, 2003).

From a policy perspective, interest in work/family issues has expanded considerably over the past decade, with colleges and universities starting to pay attention to the importance of these issues for faculty, students, and staff. Some of this interest was jump-started in 1993 when the federal government passed the Family and Medical Leave Act (FMLA). FMLA was established to protect those having families and those with significant family responsibilities that could inhibit an employee's ability to work. Organizations with fifty or more employees, as well as all public agencies, are bound by law to provide up to twelve work weeks of unpaid leave during any twelve-month period for one or more of the following reasons (U.S. Department of Labor, 2004):

- Birth and care of the newborn child of the employee
- Placement with the employee of a son or daughter for adoption or foster care
- Care for an immediate family member (spouse, child, or parent) with a serious health condition
- To take medical leave when the employee is unable to work because of a serious health problem

The vast majority of colleges and universities are bound by FMLA. This has had both negative and positive consequences for faculty combining work and family. The legislation is positive in that it safeguards faculty from losing their job and their insurance coverage when they take a leave for family reasons. It is also positive in that FMLA forces all covered institutions to consider issues associated with family leave, an issue that prior to 1993 was invisible on many campuses. It is negative, however, in that we found that some campuses do nothing else but offer FMLA provisions to new parents, which means the grant of unpaid leave. It is negative as well in that the presence of FMLA can exonerate the conscience of higher education institutions from doing more to help faculty negotiate the combination of work and family.

Aside from the passage of FMLA, there is other evidence that some campuses are recognizing that work and family concerns affect the productivity of the academic workforce, thus bringing about change in the number and types of programs designed to address these concerns for the entire campus community. As evidence of this interest, the College and University Work Family Association (CUWFA) was founded to provide "leadership in facilitating the integration of work and study with family/personal life at institutions of higher learning" (2001). CUWFA recognizes that the complexities of life can have an impact on work and learning in higher education. As further testament to the importance of this issue, the American Association of University Professors (AAUP) recommended that all academic institutions institute a policy to accommodate women with young children by stopping the tenure clock (2001). The University of Pennsylvania, for example, is in the process of creating a policy that would provide an automatic extension of the tenure clock for childbirth rather than having the extension be optional (Fogg, 2004).

While combining parenthood and faculty life is challenging for both men and women, this chapter focuses on the policy issues affecting women tenure-track faculty with young children. We focus on women because the challenges they face are exacerbated by such factors as the biological clock coinciding with the tenure clock, the physical demands of pregnancy and childbirth, the historical exclusion of women in academe, and societal expectations about motherhood (Varner, 2000; Williams, 2000). More specifically, the focus of this chapter is on how research universities accommodate the needs of tenure-track women with young children.

Negotiating Work and Family: Perspectives from the Literature

A review of the current literature on faculty, work/family issues, and institutional policy is heartening in that it reveals that postsecondary institutions are starting to deal more forthrightly with work and family concerns. Colleges and universities have implemented different kinds of policies to accommodate tenure-track faculty who have young children, ranging from basic maternity leave (paid or unpaid) to policies that allow for flexible tenure tracks. Based on a survey of chief academic officers at research universities in the mid-1990s, Raabe (1997) found that 84 percent provided unpaid maternity leave, 74 percent provided paid maternity leave, 47 percent had on-campus child care facilities, 21 percent offered financial assistance for child care, 36 percent offered accommodative scheduling to meet family needs, and 29 percent offered expansion of time for tenure for family-related reasons. A more recent survey of 256 colleges and universities indicates that research universities were the most likely of the institutional types to have family-friendly policies (see Chapter Three, this volume). The most common solutions were those without direct financial costs to the institution. For example, 86 percent of research universities offered institution-wide tenure clock stop policies, and 53 percent provided unpaid leaves in excess of FMLA. Hollenshead and colleagues (Chapter Three, this volume) also found that policies that cost more were less common. Specifically, only 22 percent of research universities in their study offered paid leave for dependent care, 32 percent offered modified duty policies for faculty (course releases), 29 percent offered reduced appointments for either extraordinary or ordinary circumstances, and approximately 22 percent allowed tenure-track faculty to have part-time appointments or to job-share. Additional findings from a national study of parental leave in higher education found that private institutions are more likely than public ones to have leave policies (Yoest, 2004). The research on leave policies indicates an awareness by institutional policymakers, especially those at research universities, that the personal lives of academics are worthy of attention.

There is also considerable research to demonstrate that postsecondary work/family policies tend to be underused by faculty (Drago and Colbeck, 2003; Finkel, Olswang, and She, 1994; Hochschild, 1997; Raabe, 1997; Ward and Wolf-Wendel, 2004; Yoest, 2004). Many policies are still too new to know if they can be used safely without hurting one's chances of earning tenure, leaving the use of such policies a risky proposition (Ward and Wolf-Wendel, 2004). Furthermore, there is research to suggest that faculty, and especially women faculty, go to great lengths to avoid being seen as "in need of assistance" while on the tenure track, which in extreme cases prevents some women faculty from having a child. Those women faculty who have children often avoid using available policies for fear of reprisal, a behavior identified as bias avoidance (Drago and others, 2004). Based on their survey of faculty at a research university, Finkel, Olswang, and She (1994) found similar results. A majority of faculty, regardless of gender, rank, and family status, supported the idea of paid leave for women faculty for childbirth and for newborn care and supported unpaid leave for ongoing infant care. A majority of faculty also supported stopping the tenure clock in these circumstances. Interestingly enough, however, these same faculty members reported that taking such a leave would hurt them professionally; as a consequence, of those surveyed who had children (almost 50 percent), only a small percentage took all of their allowable leave.

The literature suggests that a small but growing number of campuses are creating and implementing work/family policies, with research universities, as compared to other types of institutions, being most likely to have policies. And perhaps most enlightening (and problematic) is that the literature reveals that the climate of colleges and universities is such that faculty are reluctant to use existing family-friendly policies.

The purpose of this chapter is to learn more about the policy arena in research universities by examining existing policies and their use. Furthermore, we learn from women faculty who are currently on the tenure track and are mothers of young children about their views about work and family policies at research universities.

Research Design of the Study

The research reported in this chapter is part of a larger study of how not-yet-tenured women faculty at research universities attempt to achieve balance between their parental and professional roles. The focus is on how institutional context and policy availability affect the ability of these women to negotiate work and family demands. The study is guided by the following research questions:

- What work and family policies are available for faculty use?
- To what extent are these policies used?
- How do women faculty members with children view these policies?

Research Methods. The study focuses on women faculty at research universities, where faculty work is marked by the consuming challenges of research, publication, and extramural funding, in addition to teaching and service. The thirty women in the study represent a range of disciplinary backgrounds and are from nine research universities from different regions of the country, and with varying levels of prestige. The purpose in this variation lies in the potential that not all institutions are the same and factors like location and prestige might make the balance between work and family either more manageable or more precarious. Institutional prestige was determined by limiting the sample to women at research-extensive universities according to the Carnegie classification system. Second, to capture the variability within the research-extensive category, we looked at membership in the Association of American Universities (AAU) to identify top-tier research universities. Thirteen of the thirty faculty interviewed were from AAU member institutions, and the remaining seventeen were from other research-extensive institutions.

The study relies on formal interviews with women assistant professors currently making progress on the tenure track who have children under five years of age and newly promoted associate professors (promoted within the past year) who also have children under five years of age. This sample configuration supports the ultimate goal of the study: to learn more about how institutional policy affects the ability to balance work and family. Interviews were guided by a semistructured protocol with questions related to policies available on campus, the utility and use of such policies, ideas about what policies would be most helpful, and the impact of using policies in relation to tenure. In addition to interviews, we collected policy statements and other institutional documents related to work and family from the nine institutions.

Analysis Procedures.   The interviews were transcribed and then analyzed and interpreted using the constant comparative approach (Strauss and Corbin, 1990; Strauss, 1987). Data analysis of both the interviews and the documents was inductive and identified common themes and emerging patterns. With this technique "the patterns, themes, and categories of analysis come from the data; they emerge out of the data rather than being imposed on them prior to data collection and analysis" (Patton, 1980, p. 306). Qualitative methods are appropriate because the topic is rooted in women's experiences, which is best understood from the women themselves.

The data collection and analysis conform to the highest standards of qualitative research. Both researchers were involved in data collection and analysis and were in constant communication about data collected and emerging themes. Our own position as professors and mothers provides additional perspective in collecting and analyzing the data. Member checks were conducted by selecting study participants to review and analyze working themes from the data to see if they resonated with individual experience. Feedback was then incorporated into the final narrative. An audit trail was maintained through rigorous adherence to record keeping at all stages of data collection and analysis.

Findings: Policy Perspectives

As the purpose of this chapter is to learn more about the policy environment, we will not belabor the daily life experiences of these women. Information about the day-to-day challenges and sources of satisfaction for women faculty with young children is presented elsewhere (Ward and Wolf-Wendel, 2004). A brief review of those findings demonstrates some consistency with prior studies about life on the tenure track for all junior faculty members: the tenure track is a stressful time, academic work never ends, and institutional expectations for tenure can be unclear (Boice, 1992; Tierney and Bensimon, 1996). Without question, the presence of a child adds to the feelings of personal stress and workplace tension that those on the tenure track experience. At the same time, however, we also found that the presence of a child adds a perspective to academic work that we have not seen in previous research about women faculty. The research conducted on women faculty in general, and women faculty as mothers in particular, tends to look at academic structures as normative ones that are exclusive of women (Aisenberg and Harrington, 1988; Armenti, 2004). From one vantage point, our findings substantiate this, but a different vantage point shows women with children in tow successfully navigating a system that has historically been exclusive of them. Having a child creates priorities, adds perspective, and helps women to be clear about what they can do (and what they are willing to do) to succeed as a faculty member (Ward and Wolf-Wendel, 2004).

The findings from this study confirm that success as an academic mother is a combination of personal wherewithal and support, in addition to amenable institutional contexts and useful resources. With regard to policy, the findings of the content analysis reveal that institutional policies to support faculty as parents (such as parental leave and tenure clock stop policies) are available to varying degrees. We also found that the mere presence of a policy does not mean that faculty members feel free to use it. This supports existing research that addresses the culture of the workplace and how it can facilitate or inhibit the use of policies that are in place (Hochschild, 1997; Tierney and Bensimon, 1996).

The findings are presented by first providing an overview of the types of policies available at the nine research universities in this study. We then shift to the findings from the interviews that address faculty perceptions about the availability and use of policies, as well as perceptions about the departmental and institutional contexts and their impact in creating a policy environment that is either negative or positive. Themes presented in this chapter are those that cut across all participants regardless of institution and disciplinary area. Indeed, perceptions on the policy environment were remarkably uniform across the thirty interviewees in this study.

FMLA Is Offered, But Not Much Else. The content analysis of the policy documents in our study showed that all campuses mention FMLA and what it offers to employees needing family leave. Among our sample of nine institutions, this was the minimal provision offered. While the most minimal policies include only mention of FMLA provisions, the most progressive policies include leave provisions (FMLA) as well as explicit provisions for stopping the tenure clock. Interestingly, policies related to stopping the tenure clock existed in all faculty handbooks of the campuses we studied. However, stopping the tenure clock was not always mentioned in connection with having a child. It was more typically presented as an option in the event of sickness rather than for childbirth.

Although no campuses in our study offered paid parental leave, three of the nine campuses mentioned that faculty could use sick days (or vacation days where available) to cover a leave period. On one campus, faculty members on parental leave could apply for short-term disability. Campuses with more progressive policies mentioned stopping the tenure clock as part of the parental leave policy and also provided specifics of how this works (for example, tenure clock stops for the same amount of leave). We noted that none of the institutions had in writing particularly innovative policies such as those that allow for part-time tenure-track options. We found the general tenor of the leave policies to be quite vague, leaving faculty largely on their own to figure out how to use these policies. The findings of the interviews reveal more about faculty perceptions of these policies and how they were used (or not).

What Policy? Data analysis of the interviews reveals that many of the women in the study did not even know what policies were available to them. Many stated that information about policies was not communicated to them, and since no one mentioned the existence of maternity-related policies, they assumed there were none. As one respondent indicated, "I was the first person in my department at [campus] to have a child in nineteen years . . . and that is why there was such an open interpretation of the maternity leave policy." For this woman, as for many others in the study, the institutional policy (the maternity leave policy available for all women, not just faculty) granted a six-week leave. Six weeks can easily cut into a semester, which created a need to negotiate with the department chair. Given the timing of an academic semester, if a woman has a baby in February and is granted a six-week leave, this would mean the faculty member would conceivably start and end a class but miss the middle six weeks. This, of course, assumes there are no complications with the birth or the baby. Managing the time off needed to have a child was typically negotiated with the department chair without the assistance of an official policy. Nonetheless, we were surprised to learn that so many women were like one of our interviewees who explained, "I didn't even know the regulations for maternity leave and how much time you get, or how that works."

I Used the Policy, But Will It Help Me or Hurt Me? A handful of women in our study used available maternity leave policies and tenure clock stop policies when they had their children. For these women, the use of these policies was a mixed blessing. On the one hand, women found "turning back the tenure clock definitely made a difference"; on the other hand, there was concern that using the policy "would make me look less serious" or "hurt me somehow." Fear played a significant role in women considering using leave or stopping the tenure clock.

Several respondents indicated that they were fearful about the effect that taking a leave or stopping the tenure clock would have on their careers. Officially (and legally), the time one has off as part of an official leave or officially stopped tenure clock (regardless of reason) is not supposed to count as part of a faculty member's dossier when she does go up for tenure.

In practice, however, it is harder to implement and also harder to document how it does affect someone's tenure bid. One faculty member eloquently spoke to this issue:

> Statutorily you are supposed to be able to stop the tenure clock when you have kids. However, I don't think any slack is being cut based on you having kids. I personally feel like expectations here are very high. You can take the time you need to be with your kids as long as it doesn't interfere with your output at all. It is sort of your time management problem—if you want to take three months off to stay at home with your baby, that's fine, but down the road, you can't say, "I spent time with my kids and I only published four papers."

Officially this faculty member, like many others in the study, had taken a leave and slowed or otherwise stopped the tenure clock; however, it was not without repercussion or at least the fear and threat of it. Part of this fear comes from concerns about how external tenure reviewers would view the gap in productivity. Outside reviewers play a particularly important role in the evaluation of tenure-track faculty, especially at research universities. At top-tier institutions, in particular, faculty are expected to be national experts in their field by the time they go up for tenure, and the external review process is in place to contribute to the assessment of the emerging role as expert. In relationship to stopping the tenure clock, the general perception was that "people writing letters nationally, which here is the biggest weight, don't cut any slack for any reason."

The Departmental Chair Is Crucial in Setting the Tone for Policy Use. The presence of a policy is a start, yet it is how this policy is negotiated with the department head that is essential if the policy is to be used. The department head is particularly important when university parental leave policies are minimal or vague (Raabe, 1997; Chapter Three, this volume). We found that departmental-level responses to women faculty were very influential in determining whether and how policies were used. Department chairs, in particular, were critical to negotiating a workable leave, because most specifics about how the leave is implemented are determined at the departmental level. Indeed, we found the local departmental context to be essential to creating a climate where policies, if available, are free to be used. We found two types of departmental contexts: (1) those imbued with vague and reactive ideas about how to help faculty negotiate work and family, and (2) those that were creative, proactive, and open about helping faculty get what they need to help them succeed as parents and as professors.

Clearly, department heads have a lot of power when it comes to faculty using policies. For faculty members with a supportive chair, this was not a problem. A handful of participants noted their department heads were open to suggestion and accommodating. Indeed, several faculty members felt that their departments were supportive and that there was positive communication with the department chair and dean regarding policy options. In these rarer cases, perceptions about the use of leave and tenure policies were positive. As one professor indicated, "My department chair mentioned it [stopping the clock] to me because of pregnancy; she saw that for me and where I was in my career that it would be a bad idea for me *not* to take a leave and stop the clock." This same professor went on to say, "I obviously want to get tenure, but I wasn't one of those people who wanted to get it as fast as I can. . . . It's a natural step whether I get it in five years or ten years."

On campuses where policies were minimal and the department chair was not particularly creative, the power of the chair presented a greater challenge. What this meant for faculty was either doing without accommodation of any sort or the faculty member had to come up with a plan and then "sell it to the department head." Many of the department chairs mentioned by respondents were not unhelpful; they just did not seem to know how they could be of assistance. This left one faculty member in our study to wonder, "Should I take the semester off, or should other folks be responsible for this? I felt totally responsible." To be sure, faculty members themselves bear significant responsibility to figure out how work and family can be combined, yet from a policy perspective, many faculty in our study believed it was the institution's responsibility to have viable options available for women to consider and for department chairs to be aware of the policies.

New Generation Departments: A Hopeful Sign for the Future? Some of the women in our study talked about very helpful and open department chairs who lead progressive departments where family and work seemed more easily combined; we call these *new generation departments*. Although these departments are still relatively rare, some women in our study reported a shift occurring in their academic departments caused by the retirement of senior faculty and the opening of the academic labor market. The makeup of these new generation departments included senior faculty with young children, department chairs and other senior colleagues with their own grown children dealing with work and family issues, along with male faculty who are more involved with their families. Although a departmental discourse that includes work/family issues is still unusual, where it was present it made for a smoother transition between work and family for the women in the study. The general environment was more open. For example, a faculty member in such a department talks about how she handles weekend work commitments: "I have taken my son to every retreat. . . . I decided from the beginning if my department wanted me at a [department] retreat. then they get my consort and me. I didn't really ask if it was okay. . . . If you are going into my weekends and my evenings, that is time that is allocated for my family, and I am going to take as much of that with me as I can."

Other faculty mentioned departmental functions that included families and meetings scheduled specifically at times that were amenable to families. Again, these new generation department contexts were generally more open about work and family issues, in contrast to departments where faculty kept their family life invisible. These new generation departments were relatively rare among our sample, but they do suggest the importance of departmental context in making it feasible for faculty members to balance the demands of work and children more easily.

Institution-Wide Contexts Are Not Very Influential. Some suggest that it is not only the departmental context that affects women faculty and how they operate. Indeed, as the research by Raabe (1997) and Sullivan and colleagues (Chapter Three, this volume) demonstrates, it is at the institutional level that work/family policies are created and implemented. Given this research, we assumed that the institutional contexts of these nine research universities would be important to the women in our study. However, only two women mentioned institutional-level support. On one campus, the president had recently implemented an automatic tenure clock stop for everyone who takes a maternity leave (although this was not yet actually included in the policy documentation), and on another campus, it was the provost who had been particularly supportive and creative in spousal accommodation and women as mothers, resulting in an "environment that is actually pretty good." Other respondents indicated that the departmental context, not the institution-wide context, was influential in their ability to manage both work and family demands.

Analysis

Taking a leave and stopping the tenure clock, assuming they are available as options, are perceived as a risk for the women in this study, a finding substantiated elsewhere in research about women faculty (Drago and others, 2004; Drago and Colbeck, 2003; Finkel, Olswang, and She, 1994). From an organizational standpoint, we found that in traditional departments, the onus is on women to decipher the rules, many of them unwritten, as they figure out the nuances of maternity leave and tenure clock policies and how their use ultimately intersects with the tenure decision. While department chairs of the women in the study tended to be benignly helpful, they were also at a loss for how to assist these women. This left each woman to negotiate on a case-by-case basis how to deal with taking a leave, covering her courses, and other matters. Having an uncooperative department chair complicated the situation. This substantiates much of what we already know about women faculty in male-dominated (in numbers and ideology) contexts (Armenti, 2004; Tierney and Bensimon, 1996). Women, and certainly women with children, are in many ways viewed as anomalies, so that their cases must be dealt with privately. Accommodations in such a situation are "problems" to be resolved on an individual basis rather than institutionally.

In new generation departments, by contrast, the tensions of combining work and family and work and life are openly discussed, and there is more than one faculty member dealing with them. The issues are on the table, which results in a more proactive stance in dealing with how to combine private and public spheres. It is in these departments where institutions start to move beyond specifically binary constructions—man/woman, work/family, junior/senior, public/private—to a space where these constructions are blurred and made complicated by older men and women having children, single parents, grandparents caring for children, and new generations of employees having children in dual-career marriages. This makes everyone more cognizant of their multiple roles. The presence of children certainly does not automatically make things easier or smoother for departmental functioning or for individual women; however, awareness of the tensions is a first step. Higher education has a long way to go before being truly family friendly and women centered. But the women in this study who make their status as mothers visible are starting to confront the male ideology of the tenure clock and show that success can be achieved in multiple ways.

Future Directions: Policy Recommendations to Help Faculty Negotiate Work and Family

Respondents in this study were quick to make policy and climate recommendations to assist faculty who are attempting to balance work and family. The recommendations for policies from our respondents and from prior literature fall into several categories: policies that allow time off, policies that deal with tenure, policies that create services to support parents, and cultural changes to the institution that support the use of such policies. Together, these policies can help to make higher education more family friendly. We conclude this chapter with a review of these recommendations.

Time-Off or Leave Policies. Faculty members, like employees in other domains, are allowed unpaid leave for up to twelve weeks to take care of a dependent, according to the federal FMLA. As faculty members work on a schedule dictated by the length of an academic term, where semesters run sixteen weeks, it can be quite difficult to figure out how to take a leave when a child is born in the middle of a term. A six- or twelve-week leave, for example, may fall in the middle of a semester, making it difficult to arrange one's teaching. Some suggest that institutions allow faculty members to extend unpaid leave in excess of the twelve weeks required by FMLA. Another suggestion is to modify a faculty member's duties during an academic term to accommodate dependent care needs by release from teaching responsibilities during the semester. Other respondents suggest that institutions provide paid family leave of up to twelve weeks for birth or adoption for both men and women that is distinct from sick, vacation, or short-term disability leave. Paid leave, while potentially costly to the institution, may be a financial necessity for faculty, especially if they are relatively new to the career and do not have substantial savings to support themselves without pay.

Tenure-Related Policies. In addition to providing time off to care for dependents, some suggest changes to tenure policies to assist not-yet-tenured faculty who have young children. Recommendations in this domain typically do not call for the elimination of tenure, but do call for stoppage of the tenure clock for up to two years for faculty with primary or co-primary care giving responsibilities, which can be tied to taking family leave. As our respondents suggested, tenure stop policies not only need to be communicated internally, they must also be communicated to external reviewers so they do not penalize individuals for gaps in productivity during the leave period. Others suggest more radical changes to tenure, including the creation of flexible tenure clocks for academic careers that include centralized (as opposed to departmental-based) stop clock policies or extended tenure clocks. Furthermore, some have suggested that individuals on the tenure track be allowed to work part time and still be considered for tenure. The ability to move in and out between part-time and full-time employment has also been suggested.

Services to Support Faculty Parents. The most requested service to support new parents is the presence of affordable and accessible child care on campus. Faculty who are parents suggest that on-campus day care is often more focused on student accessibility than faculty or staff. Knowing that one's child is in a safe, accessible, and affordable day care environment allows faculty the ability to be more productive at work. In lieu of on-campus options, some respondents suggested that campuses provide referral for off-campus child care services and create a sick child care network.

Cultural Changes to Support Faculty as Parents. Top-level academic administrators need to do their part by setting the climate for work and family. They need to make the campus aware of shifting faculty demographics and how the presence of more women faculty (the case on most every campus) can call for the need to rethink processes like tenure-track and parental leave policies. Provosts need to make sure policies are in place and then educate deans and department chairs about their use and provide examples of how policies can work. Provosts and other senior administrators are also vital to setting the tone for the climate. Of course, this also means line items in the budget to cover adjuncts for parental leaves so department chairs are more likely to present them as an option. Gappa and McDermid (1997) suggest that institutions conduct ongoing needs assessments on work/family concerns, engage in campus dialogue about these concerns, appoint task forces to consider ways to create and implement policies, and tap into existing networks (such as the College and University Professional Association for Human Resources and College and University Family Work Association) to find solutions to deal with specific work/family situations.

Department chairs play probably the most important role in helping faculty negotiate work and family. They need to know policies, apply them fairly, and educate their faculty about their use. This education needs to be extended to those who may use the policy as well as to reviewers evaluating those who use it. Colleagues also play an important role in developing policy and creating an environment where it can be used. The faculty we focus on in this chapter are tenure-track faculty, who are new to the department and rightfully cautious in how they move forward in their decisions about having a child and then using available policies. Senior colleagues can play a mentoring role by talking about how leave works and also helping their colleagues with children to learn about and make use of available policies. Furthermore, senior colleagues are crucial to creating a climate where faculty make use of policy, as it is the senior faculty who will play an important role at tenure review time in the evaluation of junior faculty taking leave. Junior colleagues also play an important role. If fellow junior faculty begrudge their colleagues for taking a leave or stopping the tenure clock because it makes them feel that they are being treated unfairly, it creates a negative climate for those combining work and family. Department chairs need to maintain an open climate where policy issues regarding work and family are discussed in a forthright manner.

If colleges and universities expect to recruit and retain qualified and diverse faculties, work and family concerns must stay at the forefront of policy agendas. Administrators need to give greater consideration to the dilemmas posed by work/family issues for both individual faculty members and departments as a whole. Effective departments must develop useful work and family policies and create environments where such policies can be used without fear of retribution.

References

Aisenberg, N., and Harrington, M. *Women of Academe: Outsiders in the Sacred Grove.* Amherst: University of Massachusetts Press, 1988.

American Association of University Professors. "Statement of Principles on Family Responsibilities and Academic Work." 2001. http://www.aaup.org/statements/re01fam.htm.

Armenti, C. "May Babies and Posttenure Babies: Maternal Decisions of Women Professors." *Review of Higher Education,* 2004, 27(4), 211–231.

Boice, R. "Lessons Learned About Mentoring." In M. D. Sorcinelli and A. E. Austin (eds.), *Developing New and Junior Faculty.* New Directions for Teaching and Learning, no. 50. San Francisco: Jossey-Bass, 1992.

College and University Work Family Association. "Mission Statement." 2001. http://www.cuwfa.org.

Drago, B., and Colbeck, C. *Final Report from the Mapping Project: Exploring the Terrain of U.S. Colleges and Universities for Faculty and Families.* Final Report for the Alfred P. Sloan Foundation. University Park: Pennsylvania State University, 2003. http://lsir.la.psu.edu/workfam/mappingproject.htm.

Drago, R., and others. "The Avoidance of Bias Against Caregiving: The Case of Academic Faculty." Working paper 04–06, Population Research Institute, Pennsylvania State University, 2004.

Finkel, S. K., Olswang, S., and She, N. "Childbirth, Tenure, and Promotion for Women Faculty." *Review of Higher Education,* 1994, 17(3), 259–270.

Finkelstein, M. J., Seal, R. K., and Schuster, J. H. *The New Academic Generation: A Profession in Transformation.* Baltimore, Md.: Johns Hopkins University Press, 1998.

Fogg, P. "Hello . . . I Must Be Going." *Chronicle of Higher Education,* June 18, 2004, p. A10.

Gappa, J. M., and McDermid, S. M. *Work, Family, and the Faculty Career.* Washington, D.C.: American Association for Higher Education, 1997.

Hochschild, A. R. *The Time Bind: When Work Becomes Home and Home Becomes Work.* New York: Holt, 1997.

Patton, M. Q. *Qualitative Evaluation Methods.* Thousand Oaks, Calif.: Sage, 1980.

Perna, L. W. "Sex Differences in Faculty Tenure and Promotion: The Contribution of Family Ties." Paper presented at the annual meeting of the Association for the Study of Higher Education, Portland, Ore., 2003.

Raabe, P. H. "Work-Family Policies for Faculty: How 'Career-and Family-Friendly' Is Academe?" In M. A. Ferber and J. W. Loeb (eds.), *Academic Couples: Problems and Promises.* Urbana: University of Illinois Press, 1997.

Strauss, A. *Qualitative Analysis for Social Scientists.* Cambridge: Cambridge University Press, 1987.

Strauss, A., and Corbin, J. *Basics of Qualitative Research: Grounded Theory Procedures and Techniques.* Thousand Oaks, Calif.: Sage, 1990.

Tierney, W. G., and Bensimon, E. M. *Promotion and Tenure: Community and Socialization in Academe.* Albany, N.Y.: SUNY Press, 1996.

U.S. Department of Labor. "Compliance Assistance: Family and Medical Leave Act." 2004. http://www.dol.gov/esa/whd/fmla/.

Varner, A. "The Consequences of Delaying Attempted Childbirth for Women Faculty." Penn State Work-Family Initiative, 2000. http://lsir.la.psu.edu/workfam.

Ward, K. A., and Wolf-Wendel, L. E. "Academic Motherhood: Managing Complex Roles in Research Universities." *Review of Higher Education,* 2004, 27(2), 233–257.

Williams, J. "How the Tenure Track Discriminates Against Women." *Chronicle of Higher Education,* Oct. 27, 2000.

Wilson, R. "A Push to Help New Parents Prepare for Tenure Review." *Chronicle of Higher Education,* Nov. 9, 2001, p. A10.

Yoest, C. "Parental Leave in Academia." 2004. http://www.faculty.virginia.edu/familyandtenure/institutional%20report.pdf.

KELLY WARD *is assistant professor of higher education at Washington State University.*

LISA E. WOLF-WENDEL *is associate professor and coordinator of the master's program in higher education at the University of Kansas.*

5

A professor who uses a stop-the-clock policy cannot be certain that his or her total work output will be evaluated as if he or she had a normal probationary period.

Implementing Flexible Tenure Clock Policies

Saranna Thornton

There are several faculty career paths in higher education, but the path that offers the most compensation (Monks, 2004) and the most job security is a full-time appointment on the path leading from assistant professor on the tenure track, to associate professor with tenure, to full professor (also with tenure). Data collected by the American Association of University Professors (Curtis, 2005) show a multidecade pattern of disproportionate rates of promotion up the academic career ladder for female faculty relative to males.

Among female faculty, the percentage decreases at each higher rung in the career ladder. In the ladder ranks, male faculty are most concentrated at the rank of full professor and female faculty at the rank of assistant professor. (For simplicity the term *ladder ranks* will be used to refer to full-time faculty positions, either tenured or tenure track, at the ranks of assistant, associate, or full professor.) This result holds for all institutional types: research university, doctoral university, comprehensive college, and baccalaureate college. It also holds for different academic disciplines (the humanities, social sciences, and natural sciences), and it has persisted since 1972, when the 1964 U.S. Civil Rights Act's prohibitions against discrimination based on sex were extended to higher education.

Theories that women's disproportionate representation at the higher rungs of the career ladder are due to insufficient numbers of women earning

Special thanks to Hampden-Sydney College for supporting this research through the Faculty Fellowship Summer Research Fund and to Daniel Hamermesh for inspiring and guiding this research.

Ph.D.s or women "choosing" not to enter or remain in ladder-rank jobs have been discredited by data (Brown and Woodbury, 1995; Monks, 2004).

One alternative explanation, known as disparate impact discrimination, is that female faculty are evaluated for tenure and promotion under standards that appear to be neutral but have the effect of reducing women's ability to advance. As Hochschild (1975) pointed out, the tenure system and the corresponding expectations of ladder-rank faculty evolved at a time when professors were likely to be married men with stay-at-home wives who performed the work of home production, that is, all the work performed at home that is necessary to make a household run, including grocery shopping, cooking, cleaning, laundry, running errands, paying the bills, and caring for children. Thirty years later, the demands imposed on ladder-rank faculty have not changed in significant ways. Home production is still disproportionately expected of the female partner. If she also happens to be an assistant professor, the dual demands of tenure track and household will have a negative impact on her progress up the career ladder, relative to the progress of similarly qualified men.

This chapter details how the rigid, up-or-out structure of the current tenure system results in promotion decisions that have a negative impact on both the professors under review and the schools that employ them, examines how tenure clock policies could simultaneously reduce inefficiencies in the tenure system and improve the probability of promotion for female assistant professors, and analyzes the results of a survey of the actual practices of seventy-six four-year colleges and universities in the implementation of their stop the clock policies.

Inefficiencies in the Evaluation of Candidates for Tenure

For labor markets to yield outcomes that benefit both employers and employees, all parties must have accurate information regarding the quality of the labor being purchased or sold. But accurate information rarely exists.

College and university employers offering lifetime contracts to faculty want some evidence that they are tenuring people who will be productive over their career lifetimes, typically thirty to forty years. Senior colleagues thus seek to make an accurate forecast of an assistant professor's probable lifetime productivity by observing the faculty member's actual productivity during a probationary period that typically lasts five years (with the tenure decision made in the sixth year and a terminal seventh year contract offered to a professor who is denied tenure). The quality and quantity of a professor's teaching, research, and service during the probationary period thus serve as a signal to the academic institution of what to expect from the professor over the long term.

But sometimes the signals that tenure committees rely on in their decision making become contaminated and do not serve as accurate predictors of a probationary professor's probable lifetime productivity. In these situations, the ratio of "signal" to the amount of "noise" in the probationary professor's work record is too low to permit tenure committees to make accurate predictions.

Although much of the original discussion on stop-the-tenure-clock policies focused on the ways in which pregnancy and childbirth introduced noise into a probationary professor's work record, colleges and universities have come to recognize that many other events, which affect both men and women, are a potential source of noise. Although professors typically are able to return to productive teaching, research, and service after such events, one or two such events occurring during the five-year probationary period are likely to distort a professor's work record seriously.

What does a rational decision maker do in such circumstances, particularly when female faculty are more likely than males to have "noisy" probationary work records because only women give birth? Given that there are significant costs to the institution in both time and money to reentering the hiring market to replace a professor denied tenure, and given the benefits of tenuring high-quality faculty whose probationary records do not reflect their true productivity, a rational decision maker seeks some way to increase the amount of signal relative to the noise.

This does not constitute lowering tenure standards. It involves identifying ways to allow probationary professors to generate more accurate means of demonstrating the quality and quantity of their work efforts.

How Stopping the Tenure Clock Works

Stop-the-tenure-clock (STC) policies allow faculty to lengthen their pretenure, probationary periods by one or more semesters. Stanford University became one of the first institutions to permit faculty to stop the tenure clock in 1971 when it started permitting female professors to stop the tenure clock up to two times during the probationary period for the birth of a child (Bunk, 1997). Like Stanford's original policy, STC policies typically were available only to female professors who gave birth during their probationary periods. This was done in recognition that women face unusual challenges when they must coordinate pregnancy and childbirth with the pursuit of tenure—challenges that tend to lower the signal-to-noise ratio in their work records.

In 1974 the AAUP added its support for the adoption of STC policies. In its "Statement on Leaves of Absence for Child-Bearing, Child-Rearing, and Family Emergencies," the AAUP recommended that faculty who took a maternity leave or child rearing leave also be allowed to stop the tenure clock without penalty. In 2001, the AAUP modified its 1974 recommendations in its "Statement of Principles on Family Responsibilities and Academic Work." In this statement, it recommended that stopping the tenure clock be possible whether or not a leave of absence is taken; that a clock stop also be available for the adoption of a child; that only parents who are primary or coequal caregivers be allowed to stop the clock; and that extensions of the probationary period be limited to a maximum of two years. (See Rhoads and Yoest, 2004, for an explanation of why allowing secondary caregivers to stop the clock can be disadvantageous.)

In the 1990s larger numbers of colleges and universities adopted STC policies. By 1995 a study of 375 four-year colleges and universities found that 49 percent of the institutions allowed faculty to stop the tenure clock for personal reasons (Friedman, Rimsky, and Johnson, 1996). Another survey of approximately 180 four-year college and university economics departments conducted every year since 2000 shows that between 75 and 80 percent of the institutions responding in any given year have either formal or informal STC policies (Deck, Collins, and Curington, 2000, 2001, 2002, 2003, 2004).

The list of qualifying reasons for stopping the tenure clock expanded dramatically during the 1990s, as faculty and administrators came to understand that many factors besides childbirth and child rearing can introduce high levels of noise into a probationary professor's work record. Although the list of qualifying reasons varies across institutions, additional qualifying reasons now include adoption; significant elder care or dependent care responsibilities; disability or chronic illness of the professor; injured spouse or domestic partner who needs care; death of a parent, child, spouse, or domestic partner; catastrophic residential property loss (this at a university in an area frequented by hurricanes); military service; legal concerns (for example, settling an estate, processing a divorce, custody dispute, civil suit, or defense of a felony criminal charge); unavoidable delays in the completion of a research facility; natural disaster that destroys research materials; unexpected bankruptcy of a publishing company after a book has been formally accepted for publication; and periods of purely administrative duties. (Schools surveyed for this list of qualifying reasons include the University of Wisconsin, University of Michigan, Duke University, Claremont-McKenna College, Truman State University, University of Wyoming, New York University, Northwestern University, Stanford University, University of Chicago, and the University of Pennsylvania.)

Some colleges and universities allow faculty to stop the clock whether or not they also take a leave of absence and others do not. Policies also vary in the number of times the clock can be stopped—one, two, or three years or no limits at all. There is also much variation in how the tenure dossier of a professor is evaluated when the clock has been stopped—although there should not be.

Using an analogy, imagine that you are a college basketball coach who attends high school games to observe outstanding players with the goal of recruiting them. You have observed a talented athlete playing in five games. In four of the five games, the athlete scored over twenty points, but in one game scored only eight points. You also know that the player experienced an unusually stressful event before the bad game and suspect that might have temporarily interfered with the athlete's performance. Should you try to observe the athlete in one more game to confirm your suspicion? Or do you write off the time and money you spent to watch those five games and begin to search for another player to observe? If the costs in your time and money of attending another game are low compared to the costs of starting from scratch with another player, it will benefit you to see the first athlete in one more game. If the athlete again scores more than twenty points, your reasoning is confirmed, and you try to recruit that player. If the athlete performs poorly, you may seek out another player to observe.

This same logic is behind the adoption of STC policies. Suppose Professor Granger is scheduled to be evaluated for tenure in her sixth year at Potter University, based on her previous five years of work at the university. But before she reaches her tenure decision, she elects to stop the tenure clock for one year following the birth of a child (or some other qualifying event). Now she will be evaluated for tenure in her seventh year. However, to have the desired effect of separating out the signal from the noise in Professor Granger's work output, her work must be evaluated as if she had served only five years. Her tenure review committee should not expect an additional year's worth of output for the additional year on the tenure clock. Moreover, in order to obtain the most accurate forecast of Professor Granger's likely lifetime productivity, her reviewers should not ignore any quality work that she performed during the year the clock was stopped.

Returning to the basketball analogy, the coach does not average the points scored by the basketball player in all six games, but treats the eight-point game as an outlier and averages only the player's points scored in the five well-played games to forecast her likely scoring abilities. The coach also does not ignore all of the information gathered during the poorly played game. Although not scoring herself, maybe the athlete played excellent defense or helped other team members score. This positive information about the player's performance is combined with the other information to make the recruiting decision.

Another variation in how the tenure dossier of a professor is evaluated when he or she has stopped the clock involves a substantial perversion of the STC policy. An increasing body of anecdotal evidence indicates that some participants in the tenure evaluation (tenure committee members, external reviewers, department chairs, deans, and provosts) view a probationary professor's decision to stop the clock as a signal that the professor is not committed to meeting the demands of academic work. The mere decision to stop the clock causes some reviewers to negatively evaluate some or all of the tenure candidate's work record (Schneider, 2000; AAUW, 2004).

Returning to the basketball analogy, if the high school athlete who played one bad game approaches the college coach and asks her to attend a sixth game to get a more accurate picture of the athlete's true abilities, the coach does not take the request as a signal that the athlete is not serious about basketball. Similarly, tenure evaluators are wrong to presume that faculty who ask to stop the tenure clock are not serious about academia.

Implementation and Utilization of Stop-the-Tenure-Clock Policies

Although academic personnel policies may be adopted at the college or university level, implementation of those policies tends to be at the department level, with a significant amount of flexibility assumed by department chairs in exactly how policies will be applied (Wilson, 2003). With regard to STC policies, executive director C. J. Didion commented on a 1993 study conducted by the Association for Women in Science regarding the climate for women in academic science careers (Bunk, 1997). In an interview, Didion emphasized that "decisions at the department level are critical to stopping the tenure clock without penalty. What's going to be your teaching level, who is going to cover [your courses]? These are the real questions, and what we found is that you really need a supportive department chair."

Another complication in trying to understand how STC policies are implemented is that many institutions have unwritten, ad hoc faculty personnel policies (Thornton, 2003; Tillinghast-Towers Perrin, 1999). In such cases, STC policies typically are negotiated between individual professors and department chairs. This produces variations in policy access and policy content across different departments within a college or university and for individual professors within departments. In order to learn more about utilization rates and implementation of STC policies, this study makes use of survey data from individual departments in a single discipline.

In November 2003, the Center for Business and Economic Research at the University of Arkansas sent out its annual labor market survey to 371 organizations, mostly four-year colleges and universities. The center graciously added four questions regarding STC policies to the two that had been included in previous surveys (Deck, Collins, and Curington, 2000, 2001, 2002, 2003, 2004). Responses to the 2003 questionnaire came from 182 organizations, 2 of which represented nonacademic employers. Of the 182 respondents, 76 colleges and universities provided information about their STC policies: 45 doctoral universities, 10 comprehensive colleges (whose highest degree granted is typically a master's), and 21 baccalaureate colleges. (Based on the average course loads of the 7 respondents in the group of 76 that did not identify their Carnegie classification, 5 are categorized as baccalaureate colleges, 1 as a comprehensive college, and 1 as a doctoral university. Also note that the small number of comprehensive and baccalaureate colleges imposes some limits on this study.)

Survey results appear in Table 5.1. Clearly institutional type is an important determinant of the availability, utilization, and implementation of STC policies. Eighty percent or more of the doctoral universities and comprehensive colleges offer STC policies, compared to less than 50 percent of the baccalaureate colleges. In addition, among the doctoral universities and comprehensive colleges, two-thirds or more had formalized their policies, while only 23.8 percent of the baccalaureate colleges offered a formal STC policy.

Table 5.1.   Stop-the-Tenure-Clock Policies: Survey Results

Policy	Doctoral (45)	Comprehensive (10)	Baccalaureate (21)	All Types (76)
Percentage with a policy	88.9	80.0	47.6	75.0
Percentage with an informal policy[a]	17.8	10.0	9.5	14.5
Percentage with a formal policy[a]	66.7	70.0	23.8	55.3
Percentage for birth or adoption[a]	66.7	40.0	28.6	52.6
Percentage for birth only[a]	15.6	40.0	19.0	19.7
Women				
Number eligible	49	16	15	80
Number using the policy	17	3	2	22
Utilization rate	34.7%	18.8%	7.5%	27.5%
Men				
Number eligible	182	40	8	230
Number using the policy	42	1	0	43
Utilization rate	23.1%	2.5%	0%	18.7%
Number of times clock can be stopped	One: 50%, two: 43%, three: 7% (N = 14)	One: 100% (N = 4)	Two: 100% (N = 1)	One: 58%, two: 37%, three: 5% (N = 19)
Directions to tenure review committees				
Use your own judgment	60.6%	0%	50%	53.1%
Evaluate years on clock	33.3%	85.7%	25%	36.7%
Evaluate total years worked	6.1%	14.3%	25%	6.2%
Average course load per year	3.92	5.30	6.29	4.8

Note: The numbers in parentheses in the column headings refer to the number of institutions in that category in the survey.

[a]Percentages may not sum to the percentage of institutions with a policy because of missing answers to some survey questions.

Doctoral universities were much more likely than either comprehensive or baccalaureate colleges to permit the clock to be stopped for both birth and adoption of a child, with two-thirds of all doctoral institutions providing this STC option.

Data on utilization rates during the 1993–2003 time period show female faculty were more likely to use STC policies than males. And both male and female faculty at doctoral universities were more likely than faculty at the other institutional types to stop the clock, although policy use is still low.

Adoption and use of STC policies may vary across institutional types because the usefulness of the policies to individual faculty members may vary substantially across those types. Teaching is typically weighted more heavily in the evaluation of a probationary professor's work record at baccalaureate colleges, and research is relatively more important at doctoral universities. With an average annual teaching load of six courses, extending the clock following a "noise-producing" event may not be necessary for a professor at a baccalaureate college to amass the substantial number of outstanding teaching evaluations needed to demonstrate excellence in teaching. And if research demands are low, gaining an extra year on the tenure clock may not be necessary for the probationary professor to demonstrate the requisite research skills. Furthermore, delaying the tenure decision by one year also delays the substantial salary increase that often follows tenure and promotion.

For a professor at a doctoral university, the opportunity to extend the tenure clock and publish in the additional probationary year may substantially assist the pretenure professor in demonstrating the requisite research skills. Moreover, lower-quality teaching that may result during the semester or year of the noise-producing event may not need to be offset by extending the clock to build up a record of better course evaluations, because teaching ability is less heavily weighted in the tenure decision.

One of the most important findings of the survey is that a professor who uses an STC policy cannot be certain that the policy will be implemented as it is supposed to be: the professor's total work output evaluated as if he or she had a normal probationary period. Variation across institutional types is large, with only one-third of the responding doctoral universities and one-quarter of responding baccalaureate colleges instructing tenure reviewers to evaluate the probationary professor's work output properly.

Over 83 percent of comprehensive colleges did provide accurate instructions to tenure review committees. But a surprisingly large percentage of doctoral universities and baccalaureate colleges with STC policies allows internal and external reviewers to exercise their own judgment when reviewing tenure files. Consequently, some members of a tenure review committee may be evaluating the work output of the tenure candidate properly, while others improperly expect more work output for the "additional" year or more of probation. Without polling all the likely tenure reviewers before electing to stop the clock, a probationary professor at these schools has little certainty about how his or her work record will be evaluated when the tenure review is conducted. Perhaps low rates of use reflect large numbers of probationary professors exercising great caution when it comes to the decision to stop the tenure clock.

With so few colleges and universities explicitly instructing tenure reviewers on the proper method for evaluating the work record of a probationary professor who stopped the clock, STC policies are probably not accomplishing the goal of producing fairer evaluations of faculty members who experience a noise-producing event during their probationary periods. Moreover, the failure of STC policies to be properly implemented is likely to have a disproportionate impact on female faculty because they are more likely to use these policies.

Conclusion

Although discouraging, these research results do not suggest that STC policies should be abandoned. The goal of raising the signal-to-noise ratio in probationary professors' work records is still worth attaining, particularly because the benefits of achieving this goal are likely to affect female faculty disproportionately and thus help reduce their underrepresentation at the higher ladder ranks. Rather than give up on STC policies, professional academic associations (for example, the AAUP, American Association of University Women, Association for Women in Science, and Committee on the Status of Women in Economics), in concert with academic deans, should consider devoting more resources to ensuring that senior faculty (who are most likely to be tenure reviewers) know how to conduct a tenure evaluation properly when a probationary professor has elected to stop the tenure clock.

Still more changes need to be made in academia, particularly for female and male faculty who are trying to balance work and family. Drago and Williams (2000) and Williams (2000) point out that the work demands placed on ladder-rank faculty still assume that the positions are populated by individuals who have no family responsibilities or who can subcontract those responsibilities to someone else, such as a partner. But the rising percentage of full-time female faculty and an increase in the number of male faculty who expect to participate more in child rearing than did earlier generations of men mean that there is a mismatch between the demands of the jobs and the individuals who are taking those jobs. As Drago and Williams (2000) note, raising a child takes twenty years, not one semester (or one year). So while STC policies have the potential to mitigate the negative effects of short-term disruptions in a professor's work output, they are not a solution to the long-term problems that will result from the mismatch between the current demands placed on faculty in ladder-rank jobs and the desires of faculty in those jobs to balance work with family. The solution to those problems lies in a broader restructuring of academic work to make full participation in family life a realistic possibility for full-time faculty.

References

American Association of University Professors. "Statement of Principles on Family Responsibilities and Academic Work." 2001. http://www.aaup.org/statements/REPORTS/re01fam.htm.

American Association of University Women. *Tenure Denied: Cases of Sex Discrimination in Academia.* Washington, D.C.: American Association of University Women, 2004.

Brown, B. W., and Woodbury, S. A. "Gender Differences in Faculty Turnover." Staff working paper 95–34, Upjohn Institute, 1995.

Bunk, S. "Policies to Stop Tenure Clock Support Family Life." *The Scientist,* 1997, *11*(23), 1. http://www.the-scientist.com/yr1997/nov/bunk_pl_971124.html.

Colbeck, C. "So Many Roles, So Little Time." *Women in Higher Education,* 2004, *13*(7), 16–17.

Curtis, J. "Inequities Persist for Women and Non-Tenure-Track Faculty: The Annual Report on the Economic Status of the Profession." *Academe,* 2005, *91*(2).

Deck, K. A., Collins, J. T., and Curington, W. P. "Survey of the Labor Market for New Ph.D. Hires in Economics." Center for Business and Economic Research, 2000. http://www.uark.edu/depts/cberinfo/aea/.

Deck, K. A., Collins, J. T., and Curington, W. P. "Survey of the Labor Market for New Ph.D. Hires in Economics." Center for Business and Economic Research, 2001. http://www.uark.edu/depts/cberinfo/aea/.

Deck, K. A., Collins, J. T., and Curington, W. P. "Survey of the Labor Market for New Ph.D. Hires in Economics." Center for Business and Economic Research, 2002. http://www.uark.edu/depts/cberinfo/aea/.

Deck, K. A., Collins, J. T., and Curington, W. P. "Survey of the Labor Market for New Ph.D. Hires in Economics." Center for Business and Economic Research, 2003. http://www.uark.edu/depts/cberinfo/aea/.

Deck, K. A., Collins, J. T., and Curington, W. P. "Survey of the Labor Market for New Ph.D. Hires in Economics." Center for Business and Economic Research, 2004. http://www.uark.edu/depts/cberinfo/aea/.

Drago, R., and Colbeck, C. *The Mapping Project: Exploring the Terrain of U.S. Colleges and Universities for Faculty and Families.* Final report for the Alfred P. Sloan Foundation. University Park: Pennsylvania State University, 2003. http://lsir.la.psu.edu/workfam/mappingproject.htm.

Drago, R., and Williams, J. "A Half-Time Tenure Track Proposal." *Change,* 2000, *32*(6), 46–51.

Friedman, D. E., Rimsky, C., and Johnson, A. *Guide to Work Family Programs.* New York: Families and Work Institute, 1996.

Hochschild, A. R. "Inside the Clockwork of Male Careers." In F. Howe (ed.), *Women and the Power to Change.* New York: McGraw-Hill, 1975.

Monks, J. "The Relative Compensation of Contingent Faculty in Higher Education." Unpublished paper, University of Richmond, 2004.

Rhoads, S. E., and Yoest, C. "Parental Leave in Academia." 2004. http://www.faculty.virginia.edu/familyandtenure.

Schneider, A. "U. of Oregon Settles Tenure Lawsuit over Maternity Leave." *Chronicle of Higher Education,* July 21, 2000, p. A12.

Thornton, S. "Maternity and Childrearing Leave Policies for Faculty: The Legal and Practical Challenges of Complying with Title VII." *University of Southern California Review of Law and Women's Studies,* 2003, *12*(2), 161–190.

Tillinghast-Towers Perrin. *Under Managed Risk: Employment Claims Drive Rising Educational Legal Liability Occurrences and Costs.* Valhalla, N.Y.: Towers Perrin, 1999.

Williams, J. *Unbending Gender: Why Family and Work Conflict and What to Do About It.* New York: Oxford University Press, 2000.

Wilson, R. "Baby, Baby, Baby." *Chronicle of Higher Education,* Feb. 28, 2003, p. A10.

SARANNA THORNTON is Elliot Associate Professor of Economics at Hampden-Sydney College in Virginia.

6

Mothers get caught between the prescriptive image of the ideal worker and the prescriptive image of the ideal mother.

The Glass Ceiling and the Maternal Wall in Academia

Joan C. Williams

The glass ceiling in academia is well documented. Women are more likely than men to end up in non-tenure-track positions. Women on tenure track are less likely than men to be at four-year institutions. And highly ranked four-year institutions tend to employ low percentages of women (Mason and Goulden, 2002). Why?

Part of the problem is gender bias, of two types. The more familiar is the glass ceiling that prevents successful women from reaching the summit of their professions. But what exactly is the glass ceiling? Typically, it is defined demographically, by documenting the dearth of women at the top. But *why* the dearth of women, when most academics (men as well as women) see themselves as committed to gender equality? Little information surfaces to help academic administrators who are determined to give women a fair shake.

Many women never get near the glass ceiling because of a type of gender bias that has only recently been documented. In a 2003 law review article, a coauthor and I documented the "maternal wall" that inhibits women's progress once they become mothers (Williams and Segal, 2003). Mason and her team also have documented the sharp impact of having children on academic women's careers. Women who have children soon after receiving their Ph.D. are much less likely to achieve tenure than men who have children at the same point in their career. Prestigious research universities tend to grant tenure to men at a much higher rate, relegating women to second-tier teaching and adjunct positions (Mason and Goulden, 2002). The result is that most women who earn Ph.D.s never get near tenure, much less tenure at a leading institution.

New Directions for Higher Education, no. 130, Summer 2005 © Wiley Periodicals, Inc.

Like the glass ceiling, the maternal wall is documented demographically by documenting the dearth of mothers in tenure-track positions or in tenure-track positions at elite universities. What triggers the maternal wall? How does it affect mothers? Again, depressing demography does not give us guidance on how to avoid more depressing demography in the future.

This chapter does. It describes the patterns of stereotyping and gender bias that create the glass ceiling and the maternal wall. After a review of over a hundred studies, I present the latest findings of empirical social psychology in a readily usable form.

Preliminaries

Most people know what stereotyping is—or think they do. The "common-sense" view represents the latest in academic psychology, circa 1950. Take the example of an employer who assumes that because, demographically, mothers as a group cut back their hours after they have children, a particular woman will do so. Sometimes called statistical discrimination, this is one type of stereotyping.

But it is only one. *Prescriptive stereotyping* is different: it does not just assume stereotypical behavior; it tries to require it (Burgess and Borgida, 1999). Sometimes prescriptive stereotyping is hostile, as when an employer tells a mother that she should not return to work because children need their mothers at home. Sometimes it is benevolent, as when an employer sends a new mother home promptly at 5:00 P.M. because "she has a baby to take care of" but keeps a new father working late because "he has a family to support" (Williams and Segal, 2003, p. 95). Good intentions do not excuse this type of gender bias, which polices men as well as women into traditional gender roles.

What economists call "statistical discrimination," social psychologists call "descriptive stereotyping." When an employer disadvantages women because of the assumption that they will conform to stereotype (as opposed to the assumption that they should), what is often involved is *cognitive bias,* the term associated with the insight that much gender bias (and race and other types of bias) stems from the ways in which stereotypes shape perception, memory, and inferences:

• *Perception.* Cognitive bias shapes the way people are perceived, as when a lawyer who returned from maternity leave was given paralegal work and responded, "I want to say, 'Look, I had a baby, not a lobotomy'" (Williams, 2000, p. 69). Once stereotypes are triggered, people's perceptions are shaped by them, and inconsistent information tends to be ignored (Heilman, 1995).

• *Memory:* People are more likely to remember stereotype-consistent behavior and to forget stereotype-inconsistent behavior (Krieger, 1995). This recall bias causes them to selectively remember events that confirm stereotypes and forget events that disconfirm them (Banaji, Hardin, and Rothman, 1993).

- *Inferences:* Stereotypes also influence inferences. Said one mother, "Before I went part-time, when people called and found I was not at my desk, they assumed that I was elsewhere at a business meeting. But after I went part-time, the tendency was to assume that I was not there because of my part-time schedule even if I was out at a meeting" (Williams and Segal, 2003, p. 97). When this mother worked full time, coworkers attributed her absences to business reasons. After she went part time, coworkers attributed her absences to family reasons.

In ambiguous situations, stereotypes often drive inferences (Krieger, 1995). Attribution, the process by which people arrive at causal explanations for social events (Travis, 1976), feeds into evaluations, which may also be influenced by inferences ("attribution bias") (Hunt, Borgida, Kelly, and Burgess, 2002). In a circular process, stereotypes drive attribution, which reinforces the stereotypes (Hamilton and Rose, 1980). This circularity accounts for the resiliency of stereotypes and the need for academic institutions to intervene.

Stereotypes often produce relatively small differences, but these add up over time. According to social psychologist Virginia Valian (1999, p. 142), "Success is largely the accumulation of advantage, exploiting small gains to get bigger ones." One experiment set up a model that built in a tiny bias in favor of promoting men; after a while, 65 percent of top-level employees were male. This accumulation of disadvantage plays an important role in creating the glass ceiling and the maternal wall—and especially the interaction of the two.

The Glass Ceiling

One-half of the glass ceiling involves scenarios that cause women to feel they have to try twice as hard to achieve half as much. One such scenario is when a woman says something clever at a meeting, only to hear it recalled later and attributed to a male colleague who had repeated it. The other half of the glass ceiling involves scenarios in which high-powered women are penalized for doing their jobs too well. An example of this is when a leading journal agrees to publish a woman's article, and some of her colleagues begin talking about her arrogance rather than her accomplishment.

Why Women Have a Harder Time Establishing Competence. Social status predicts perceived competence. Typically, men, as measured by body language and patterns of deference in controlled laboratory settings, are accorded more status than women (Foschi, 2000). Women's successful performances tend to be more closely scrutinized and then assessed by stricter standards than men's. Men also have to give more convincing demonstrations of incompetence in order to be judged incompetent overall. Thus, women have to "jump through more hoops" to establish themselves (Biernat and Kobrynowicz, 1997, p. 544).

One study of academia shows that after controlling for scholarly productivity, women attain tenure more slowly than men do. This slower development cannot be accounted for by a lower standard of performance. Women actually publish higher-quality work than men do, as measured by the number of times their work is cited by other scholars (Hewlett, 2002).

Another question is why women end up doing tasks that subtract from their time for research, such as more student counseling, local arrangements for conferences, and arranging faculty teas or holiday parties. One study found that men who believed that they were interacting with a woman were more likely to assign their partner feminine tasks (Eagly, Wood, and Diekman, 2000). Although taking on such tasks is not the fast track to power and authority, refusing them may lead to charges that a woman is "uncollegial."

There are a number of ways in which subtle gender stereotyping makes it more difficult for women to demonstrate their competence:

• *Competency stereotypes affect objective rule application.* The struggle to establish competence is inhibited by both the application and the structure of objective rules. Studies have shown that when applying objective rules, colleagues tend to create exceptions for men or give them the benefit of the doubt, whereas women are held to the universalistic standards. Social psychologists call this "in-group favoritism" or "leniency bias" (Brewer, 1996, p. 65). Leniency bias is important because it focuses attention not only on the deferential treatment of women but also on the preferential treatment of men (Taylor, 1981). To quote Brewer (1996, p. 65), "Coldly objective judgment seems to be reserved for members of out-groups." Highlighting women's failures while glossing over those of men makes it harder for women to establish their competence. "Selection and merit reviews are particularly vulnerable" to leniency bias.

• *Women are judged on their accomplishments, men on their potential.* Actors tend to attribute their own behavior, or that of their in-group, to stable causes and attribute the behavior of out-groups to situational causes: he is brilliant, but she just got lucky (Deaux and Emswiller, 1974). In academia, men tend to be judged on their potential: he does not have enough publications, but he shows such promise we should at least invite him to give a job talk. Women tend to be judged strictly on their accomplishments: "We can't interview her; she's unqualified" (Krieger, 1995).

• *Women's mistakes are remembered long after men's are forgotten.* Facts that fit a given stereotype are more accurately recalled than facts that do not (Heilman, 1995). Members of the in-group are more likely to recall undesirable behavior committed by out-group members than by in-group members (Krieger, 1995). As a result, women may have a harder time than men being perceived as competent because their mistakes are remembered after men's are forgotten.

• *Results of the competency struggle.* The struggle to be perceived as competent affects women in multiple ways. First, as members of the out-group, they tend to receive fewer rewards than men (Brewer, 1996). In one study, when an in-group member outperformed an out-group member, the in-group wanted to divvy awards based on equity (with awards tied to percentage produced); when an out-group member outperformed an in-group member, in-group members wanted to divvy awards based on equality (identical percentages regardless of individual production figures) (Eagly and Karau, 2002).

In addition, in workplaces with few women, studies show that token women tend to experience polarized evaluations—either very good or very bad (Farley, 1996; Krieger, 1995). A few superstars may actually be perceived as more competent than similarly situated men (Heilman, 2001). But most women tend to experience very low evaluations. This pattern is especially relevant to student teaching evaluations. In addition to polarized evaluations, token women often experience what social psychologists call the "solo effect" (Biernat and others, 1998, p. 304), causing them to feel isolated and unhappy (Taylor, 1981). Of course, social isolation can easily give rise to poor evaluations because a worker is out of the loop.

Third, according to Taylor (1981), in environments where women experience bias, particularly those where they are outnumbered, women sometimes can succeed only by stepping into roles reassuring to men. These include the *mother,* a nurturing consoler who handles the emotion work of a group; the *princess,* who pairs with a male protector; the *pet,* "a group mascot who applauds male achievements and gains acceptance by being a cute little person"; or *Ms. Efficiency,* a glorified secretary who organizes the group. Of course, glorified secretaries are not typically considered to be high-powered academics; nor may they have the time to meet the objective requirements for tenure or promotion.

The struggle for competence may be twice as difficult for women of color. The work of Ridgeway and Smith-Lovin (1999) helps explain the "concrete wall" faced by women of color, positing that a person's different statuses are additive. Thus, a woman of color will have to overcome the additive effect of negative assumptions triggered by her race *and* negative assumptions triggered by her gender (Kennelly, 1999).

Catch-22: When Women Are Penalized for Being Too Competent. While women often have more trouble being perceived as competent than men do, they also may be penalized if they are too competent. To quote Heilman (1995, p. 16), "Women in non-traditional fields may be penalized if they do their jobs well—in some cases, because they do their jobs well." Women face a catch-22.

Heilman also found that women judged as "successful" often triggered dislike. A study of women managers found that they were found to be described as "bitter, quarrelsome and selfish . . . [with] an unbridled ambition for power and achievement" (Heilman, Block, Martell, and Simon, 1989, p. 941). Whereas assertiveness in men will often be seen as evidence of brilliance or originality, similar behavior in women may be seen as distasteful. To Taylor (1981, p. 103), "Cognitively, it may matter little whether a person categorizes a bright, successful female as a 'career woman' or a 'castrating bitch,' but on both the practical and the motivational side, it will matter a great deal."

Negative reactions to assertive women matter because "advancement in organizations depends not only on competence assessments but also on social acceptance and approval, and the negativity that is a likely reaction to women who prove themselves to be competent in areas that traditionally are off limits to them can be lethal when they strive to get ahead" (Heilman, 2001, p. 661). Thus, accomplished women find themselves on the defensive. In at least one case, a woman was denied full professorship in part for lack of collegiality (*Sweeney* v. *Board of Trustees of Keene State College,* 1979).

As noted above, women who are willing to follow feminine stereotypes may thrive in departments where other women do not. However, women who do conform to stereotypes may well become vulnerable for that reason. For example, in *Weinstock* v. *Columbia University* (2000), the plaintiff was faulted for behaving in too feminine a manner. As the dissent explained, "by describing her as 'nice' and referring to her nurturing manner, [colleagues] were not extolling her positive qualities—rather, they were using these qualities to highlight what they perceived to be her intellectual weakness" (p. 53).

Another danger of traditionally feminine behavior is that if a woman plays the warm and nurturing role, she may find herself doing a disproportionate amount of student advising, only to have her colleagues attribute that workload to her "maternal instinct" rather than to public spiritedness; a catch-22 emerges when a department brands as uncollegial any woman who resists such work but does not value any woman who does it. Some high-powered women attempt to thwart glass ceiling catch-22s by leveraging their sexuality. An article in *Fortune* focused on women who receive approval for conforming to prescriptions of warmth and sexuality (Sellers, 1996). The women were successful because they melded masculine, assertive behavior seamlessly with "socio-emotional 'softeners' [that] assuage[d] resistance and increase[d] their influence in the group" (p. 42). In this way, a high-powered woman may "attract attention to her actual competence." However, these women perpetuate the status quo by reaffirming the unspoken requirement that women be feminine and likable.

Stereotypes become self-fulfilling, as Deaux and Major (1987) explained, when people alter their identities in order to increase approval. The warm reception women get for fulfilling others' expectations encourages women to adopt similar behavior in future interactions (Glick and Fiske, 2001). This reaffirms that women often adopt an approved feminine subtype in order to succeed.

In some sexist environments, the women who succeed are the ones who "know their place." Keeping one's place "involves downplaying the competence and behaving in a friendly, deferential manner when interacting with members of the dominant group" (Glick and Fiske, 1999, p. 209). This creates particular problems in academia. With competition intense for academic jobs, women often face a catch-22. If they act brilliant, they may fail to meet the unarticulated expectation that women will be sociable and reassuring. If they highlight their accomplishments, they may be tripped up by gendered norms of self-promotion—what is considered in a man to be "knowing his own worth" may be seen as unseemly self-promotion in a woman (Eagly and Karau, 2002).

A final disturbing pattern in academia in heavily male departments such as the hard sciences is the sexual harassment of women (Schultz, 1990; *Lipsett* v. *University of Puerto Rico,* 1988). Senior women may find themselves subjected to sexual harassment as a way of derailing them as competitors.

The Maternal Wall

Far fewer studies have explored the patterns of bias and stereotyping that affect mothers in particular as opposed to women in general. Maternal wall bias tends to be triggered at any point when maternity becomes salient—when a woman announces her pregnancy, begins to look pregnant, requests parental leave, stops the clock, or seeks a modified schedule (Williams and Segal, 2003).

In the maternal wall context, women may experience benevolent as well as hostile prescriptive stereotyping. Benevolent stereotyping polices women into traditionalist roles in a "kinder and gentler" way. After women have children, some find themselves advised to work shorter hours or to eschew travel so they can spend more time with their families.

It is one thing for an employer to be sensitive to a woman's new responsibilities—and quite another for a woman to feel that she must live up to her colleagues' expectation that she play June Cleaver.

"But I meant well." What is a well-meaning chair or other administrator to do? Ask. Some mothers have husbands at home full time and want to work long hours. Others are primary caregivers with husbands who travel and want more restricted schedules. Ask a new mother what she wants rather than making assumptions (Williams and Segal, 2003). By policing couples into stereotypical gender roles, colleagues not only rely on traditional stereotypes; they help create them. That is not a proper role for an employer, and it does not take much imagination to envision situations where legal liability might result.

In addition to negative stereotyping, mothers encounter negative competence assumptions. Work by Fiske and Glick documents that subjects rate "businesswomen" as high in competence, close to "businessmen" and "millionaires." "Housewives," in sharp contrast, are rated as very low in competence, alongside the elderly, blind, "retarded," and "disabled" (to quote the stigmatized words used by the researchers; Fiske, Cuddy, Glick, and Xu, 2002, p. 878). A more recent study found that "working mothers" are rated as more similar in competence to "housewives" than to "businesswomen" (Cuddy, Fiske, and Glisk, forthcoming). Thus, when women return from maternity leave, they may fall from "businesswoman" to "housewife" in the eyes of supervisors and colleagues.

One study found that performance reviews of female managers plummeted after pregnancy, in part because pregnancy triggers the stereotype of women as irrational and overly emotional (Halpert, Wilson, and Hickman, 1993). A 1990 study by Corse found that some people like "pregnant women better when they behave passively than when they behave assertively and evaluate them more favorably when they occupy a stereotypically feminine rather than masculine work role" (p. 40). Some coworkers also expect pregnant women to conform rigorously to the mandates of traditional femininity: to be "nonauthoritarian, easy to negotiate with, gentle, and neither intimidating nor aggressive, and nice" (p. 49). In addition to triggering negative competence assumptions, colleagues may sanction mothers who behave in traditionally masculine ways due to an unspoken expectation that mothers will be nonthreatening and "nice."

Another major issue is attribution bias. Among the most common effects of maternal wall attribution bias is the perception that when a mother is absent or late for work, she is caring for her children, while a similarly situated father is thought to be researching (Kennelly, 1999). Employers concerned about women's advancement have recognized the challenges of this type of attribution bias. For example, one hypothetical used by Deloitte and Touche for discussion purposes involved a man and a woman who were late for an early morning meeting. While the team joked about, and then forgot, the man's late arrival, they assumed the woman's late arrival reflected child care difficulties; after the meeting, the team leader warned her of the need to rethink her priorities (McCracken, 2000).

Deloitte's example dramatizes the potentially corrosive impact of maternal wall attribution bias. Another example of attribution bias was the mother, quoted above, who switched from full time to part time and reported that when she was working full time and her colleagues found her not at her desk, they did not hold it against her because they attributed her absence to business reasons. After she went part time, they did tend to hold it against her when they found she was not at her desk, because they attributed her absence to her part-time schedule (even if she was at a business function):

> Before I went part-time, people sort of gave me the benefit of the doubt. They assumed that I was giving them as fast a turnaround as was humanly possible. After I went part-time, this stopped, and they assumed that I wasn't doing things fast enough because of my part-time schedule. As a result, before I went part-time, I was getting top-of-the-scale performance reviews. Now I'm

not, though as far as I can tell, the quality of my work has not changed
[Williams and Segal, 2003, p. 97].

Note that this lawyer enjoyed the benefit of the doubt as long as
she worked full time. Once she went part time, the "leniency bias" no
longer worked in her favor.

The 1993 Family and Medical Leave Act requires that academic institutions offer unpaid parental leaves to primary caregivers. Many universities also offer stop-the-clock policies, and some are beginning to offer
reduced-hours tenure tracks. However, studies by Hochschild (1997) report
that women who use family-friendly policies often suffer career detriments
because of negative competence assumptions associated with motherhood.
For example, a study by Eagly and Steffen (1986) found that women who
work part time are viewed as less warm and nurturing than homemakers
but as having the same lack of go-getter qualities.

A related phenomenon is the widespread sense that certain (typically
dead-end) jobs are suitable for mothers, whereas certain (typically high-
powered) jobs are not (Heilman, 1983). The perceived lack of fit between
good jobs and mothers is another facet of the maternal wall.

Mothers also can experience the catch-22 between being an ideal
worker and an ideal mother. Employed mothers are perceived as less family oriented, more selfish, and less sensitive to the needs of others than
unemployed mothers (Etaugh and Gilomen, 1989). A mother's decision to
remain employed, unlike a father's, is perceived as uncorrelated with her
desire to "provide," according to studies by Biernat and Kobrynowicz
(1997). In the same series of studies, the "very good mother" was more
likely than the "very good father" to be described as "willing to always be
there and to do anything for the children" (p. 592).

Mothers get caught between the prescriptive image of the 24/7 ideal
worker and the prescriptive image of the 24/7 ideal mother (Ridgeway and
Correll, 2004). Because no one can serve two masters 24/7, the result is a
clash between the ideal-worker norm and the norm of parental care, which
gives rise to the "hard truth" that a woman cannot be a good worker and
a good mother (Williams, 2000).

Sociological evidence reveals that mothers sometimes experience
informal social sanctions for violating the prescriptive norm of the ever-
available mother. "It takes more than paying a mortgage to make a home,"
said one woman's colleague disapprovingly when she returned from maternity leave (Hochschild, 1997, pp. 106–107). Also, in one tenure denial
lawsuit involving a reported tentative settlement of $495,000, the provost
who denied tenure allegedly told another professor that the mother's decision to "stop the clock" was a "red flag"; the department chair also wrote
in a memo that she "knew as a mother of two infants, she had responsibilities that were incompatible with those of a full-time academician."
(Schneider, 2000).

The incidence of childlessness among women academics is high. Over 50 percent of tenured women have no children (Mason and Goulden, 2002). The result is that women academics are more likely than women in many other fields to find themselves isolated. This gives rise to a version of the solo effect, discussed earlier, where the few-and-far-between mothers feel isolated and out of the loop. Mothers may be so few that any mistake a mother makes is heightened in salience.

Unfortunately, very few studies have examined stereotypes related to women of color and motherhood. Yet evidence is emerging of distinctive stereotypes of professional African American mothers. An important dissertation by Clarke (2002) documents that the maternal wall for black women professionals deprives many not only of children but also of partners. African American women in positions of power are much less likely to find partners: in effect, many black women professionals hit a "family wall" rather than a maternal wall. More research is needed.

The Interaction Between the Glass Ceiling and the Maternal Wall

Because the ideal worker in academia continues to be defined as someone who needs no time off for family care, most parents find themselves in the position of "asking for accommodations" (Williams and Segal, 2003). To "gain accommodations," mothers need to be in a position where they can "cash in their chips" in order to garner political support for the accommodation proposed. If a woman has encountered glass ceiling problems, she may well have few chips to cash in: in fact, she may well find that she lacks the political support necessary to persuade people to "do her a favor." This is the most obvious way the glass ceiling exacerbates the maternal wall.

A more subtle interaction between the glass ceiling and the maternal wall occurs in careers, particularly in academia, where, it is said, "if you want to move up, you have to move." In that context, nonmothers (including men) will tend to move up if they reach a certain level of accomplishment, whereas mothers are more likely than others to be unable to relocate, according to a long line of studies (Bielby and Bielby, 1992; Deitch and Sanderson, 1987; Shauman and Xie, 1996).

Gender Wars

The maternal wall not only affects mothers; it also affects nonmothers to the extent that employers presume that all women eventually will become mothers (Heilman, 1995). For example, in *Barbano* v. *Madison County* (1990), an employer asked women applicants questions about their family lives that he did not ask men. The questions were relevant, he said, "because he did not want to hire a woman who would get pregnant and quit" (p. 141).

Another way the maternal wall disserves all women is by pitting non-mothers against mothers in a workplace (Williams, 2000). This, of course, decreases women's ability to work together to counter glass ceiling bias. Extensive anecdotal reports suggest that this division often makes women their own worst enemies, as women without children lead the charge against mothers (Burkett, 2000). These gender wars are particularly acute in academia because of the high numbers of childless women.

Childless women are understandably pained when they are asked to countenance a shift in workplace norms that would make it easier for women to have children. This wistfulness can easily turn to anger if they are asked, for example, to take over for a colleague out on parental leave, if they felt that they sacrificed having a baby themselves through what Hewlett (2002) called a "creeping nonchoice."

Childless women are often joined by child-free women. The motivations of child-free women are quite different. They never wanted children; instead, their goal is to imagine a full adult female life without children. They may feel that policies that help mothers serve to reinforce the perception that all women are mothers, which feeds the perception that women without children are unnatural.

It is important to recognize that the maternal wall often manifests as a fight among women. That does not mean that it is not gender discrimination: empirical social psychology has shown clearly that women as well as men hold gender stereotypes (Rudman, 1998). In the recent landmark maternal wall case of *Back* v. *Hastings on Hudson* (2004), the defendants were women who engaged in descriptive stereotyping, refusing to grant tenure to a school psychologist based on the assumption that she would slack off after tenure because she had "little ones at home." Prescriptive stereotyping is also a possibility: imagine a supervisor who stayed home with her children and then fails to promote another mother based on her belief that moms should work at most part time when children are young. The crucial point is that all women, nonmothers as well as mothers, are disadvantaged by a workplace that enshrines the ideal worker who starts to work in early adulthood and works, full time and over time, for forty years straight.

Fathers on the Front Lines of Family Care: The Paternal Wall

The maternal wall applies not only to mothers, but to any adult who engages in the kinds of family caregiving traditionally allocated to mothers. Unfortunately, few studies analyze the employment barriers faced by fathers who seek an active role in family care (Malin, 1998; Cunningham, 2001). More research is urgently needed on this subject.

Fathers may well face a threshold effect. Because men are presumed competent simply because they are men, fathers who take off for the occasional doctor's appointment may actually benefit at work if they are judged to be warm as well as competent (Fiske, 1999). However, if a man goes beyond the occasional school play and asks to go on a flexible work arrangement or part time, he may find his evaluations plummeting. In fact, fathers who work part time may find themselves worse off than mothers who work part time: male part-timers are perceived as "even lower in agency than the male homemaker," presumably based on the assumption that the male part-timer is an incompetent worker who cannot find a good job (Eagly and Steffen, 1986; Etaugh and Fogler, 1998).

In addition, given the widespread sense that "masculinity [is tied] to the size of a paycheck" (Gould, 1974), a father who takes time off or goes part time may face the sense that he is less of a man or inappropriately feminine. Finally and most painfully, a father whose ideal worker status is threatened may be seen not only as a less manly man but also as a less effective provider—and consequently as a flawed father (Townsend, 2002).

A dramatic example of prescriptive stereotyping of fathers is *Knussman* v. *Maryland* (2001), in which a Maryland state trooper was told that he could not take parental leave after the birth of his child "unless [his] wife [was] in a coma or dead" (p. 630). Of course, when fathers are precluded from taking time off, the result is not only to police fathers into traditional breadwinner roles; women also are policed into caregiver roles.

Conclusion

The glass ceiling and the maternal wall affect women and men in nontraditional roles in all professions. Academia, despite its lofty ivory towers, is not immune from gender stereotyping and cognitive bias. In order to combat the negative effects of stereotyping and create a more equitable workplace, academic administrators must examine each employment practice for the telltale signs of workplace discrimination exposed by the studies discussed in this chapter and many more like them.

References

Back v. *Hastings on Hudson*, 2004 U.S. App. Lexis 6684 (2d Cir. Apr. 7, 2004).

Banaji, M. R., Hardin, C., and Rothman, A. "Implicit Stereotyping in Personal Judgment." *Personality and Social Psychology*, 1993, *65*, 272–281.

Barbano v. *Madison County*, 922 F.2d 139 (2d Cir. 1990).

Bielby, W. T., and Bielby, D. D. "I Will Follow Him: Family Ties, Gender Role Beliefs, and Reluctance to Relocate for a Better Job." *American Journal of Sociology*, 1992, *97*, 1241–1267.

Biernat, M., and Kobrynowicz, D. "Gender- and Race-Based Standards of Competence: Lower Minimum Standards by Higher Ability Standards for Devalued Groups." *Journal of Personality and Social Psychology*, 1997, *72*, 544–557.

Biernat, M., and others. "All That You Can Be: Stereotyping of Self and Others in a Military Context." *Journal of Personality and Social Psychology*, 1998, *75*, 301–317.

Brewer, M. B. "In-Group Favoritism: The Subtle Side of Intergroup Discrimination." In D. M. Messick and E. Tenbrunsel (eds.), *Codes of Conduct: Behavioral Research into Business Ethics.* New York: Russell Sage Foundation, 1996.

Burgess, D., and Borgida, E. "Who Women Are, Who Women Should Be: Descriptive and Prescriptive Gender Stereotyping in Sex Discrimination." *Psychology, Public Policy, and the Law*, 1999, *5*, 665–692.

Burkett, E. *The Baby Boon: How Family-Friendly America Cheats the Childless.* New York: Free Press, 2000.

Clarke, A. Y. "I Do If I Could: Marriage, Meaning and the Social Reproduction of Inequality." Unpublished doctoral dissertation, University of Pennsylvania, 2002.

Corse, S. J. "Pregnant Managers and Their Subordinates: The Effects of Gender Expectations on Hierarchical Relationships." *Journal of Applied Behavioral Science*, 1990, *26*, 25.

Cuddy, A.J.C., Fiske, S. T., and Glick, P. "Working Moms Can't Win: Mothers Are Incompetent and Career Women Are Unkind." *Journal of Social Issues*, forthcoming.

Cunningham, K. "Father Time: Flexible Work Arrangements and the Law Firm's Failure of the Family." *Stanford Law Review*, 2001, *53*, 967–1008.

Deaux, K., and Emswiller, T. "Explanations for Successful Performance on Sex-Linked Tasks: What Is Skill for the Male Is Luck for the Female." *Journal of Personality and Social Psychology*, 1974, *29*, 80–85.

Deaux, K., and Major, B. "Putting Gender into Context: An Interactive Model of Gender-Related Behavior." *Psychology Review*, 1987, *94*, 369–389.

Deitch, C. H., and Sanderson, S. W. "Geographic Constraints on Married Women's Careers." *Work and Occupation*, 1987, *14*, 616–634.

Eagly, A. H., and Karau, S. J. "Role Congruity Theory of Prejudice Toward Female Leaders." *Psychological Review*, 2002, *109*(3), 573–598.

Eagly, A. H., and Steffen, V. J. "Gender Stereotypes, Occupational Roles, and Beliefs About Part-Time Employees." *Psychology of Women Quarterly*, 1986, *10*, 242–262.

Eagly, A. H., Wood, W., and Diekman, A. "Social Role Theory of Sex Differences and Similarities: A Current Appraisal." In T. Eckes and H. M. Trautner (eds.), *The Development of Social Psychology of Gender.* Mahwah, N.J.: Erlbaum, 2000.

Etaugh, C., and Fogler, D. "Perceptions of Parents Whose Work and Parenting Behaviors Deviate from Role Expectations." *Sex Roles*, 1998, *39*, 215–223.

Etaugh, C., and Gilomen, G. "Perceptions of Mothers: Effects of Employment Status, Marital Status, and Age of Child." *Sex Roles*, 1989, *20*, 67.

Farley, C. F. "Confronting Expectations: Women in the Legal Academy." *Yale Journal of Law and Feminism*, 1996, *8*, 333–358.

Fiske, S. T. "(Dis)respecting Versus (Dis)liking; Status and Interdependence Predict Ambivalent Stereotypes of Competence and Warmth." *Social Issues*, 1999, *55*, 473–490.

Fiske, S. T., Cuddy, A. J., Glick, P., and Xu, J. "A Model of (Often Mixed) Stereotype Content: Competence and Warmth Respectively Follow from Perceived Status and Competition." *Personality and Social Psychology*, 2002, *82*, 878–902.

Foschi, M. "Double Standards for Competence: Theory and Research." *Annual Review of Sociology*, 2000, *26*, 21–42.

Glick, P., and Fiske, S. "Sexism and Other 'Isms': Interdependence, Status, and the Ambivalent Context of Stereotypes." In W. B. Swann Jr., J. H. Langlois, and L. A. Gilbert (eds.), *Sexism and Stereotypes in Modern Society: The Gender Science of Janet Taylor Spence.* Washington, D.C.: American Psychological Association, 1999.

Glick, P., and Fiske, S. "Ambivalent Stereotypes as Legitimizing Ideologies: Differentiating Paternalistic and Envious Prejudice." In J. T. Yost and B. Major (eds.), *The Psychology of Legitimacy: Emerging Perspectives on Ideology, Justice, and Intergroup Relations.* Cambridge: Cambridge University Press, 2001.

Gould, R. "Measuring Masculinity by the Size of a Paycheck." In J. Pleck and J. Sawyer (eds.), *Men and Masculinity.* Englewood Cliffs, N.J.: Prentice Hall, 1974.

Halpert, J., Wilson, M., and Hickman, J. "Pregnancy as a Source of Bias in Performance Appraisals." *Journal of Organizational Behavior*, 1993, *14*, 649.

Hamilton, D. L., and Rose, T. L. "Illusory Correlation and the Maintenance of Stereotypic Beliefs." *Journal of Personality and Social Psychology,* 1980, *39,* 832.

Heilman, M. "Description and Prescription: How Gender Stereotypes Prevent Women's Ascent Up the Organizational Ladder." *Social Issues,* 2001, *57,* 657–674.

Heilman, M., Block, C., Martell, R., and Simon, M. "Has Anything Changed? Current Characterizations of Men, Women and Managers." *Journal of Applied Psychology,* 1989, *74,* 935–942.

Heilman, M. E. "Sex Bias in Work Settings: The Lack of Fit Model." *Research in Organizational Behavior,* 1983, *5,* 269–298.

Heilman, M. E. "Sex Stereotypes and Their Effects in the Workplace: What We Know and What We Don't Know." *Gender in the Workplace: A Special Issue of the Journal of Social Behavior and Personality,* 1995, *10,* 3–26.

Hewlett, S. A. *Creating a Life: Professional Women and the Quest for Children.* New York: Talk Miramax Books, 2002.

Hochschild, A. *The Time Bind: When Work Becomes Home and Home Become Work.* New York: Holt, 1997.

Hunt, J. S., Borgida, E., Kelly, K., and Burgess, D. "The Scientific Status of Research on Gender Stereotyping." In D. L. Faigman, D. H. Kaye, M. J. Saks, and J. Sanders (eds.), *Modern Scientific Evidence: The Law and Science of Expert Testimony.* St. Paul, Minn.: West, 2002.

Kennelly, I. "'That Single Mother Element': How White Employers Typify Black Women." *Gender and Society,* 1999, *13,* 168–192.

Knussman v. *Maryland,* 272 F.3d 625 (4th Cir. 2001).

Krieger, L. H. "The Content of Our Categories: A Cognitive Bias Approach to Discrimination and Equal Employment Opportunity." *Stanford Law Review,* 1995, *47,* 1161.

Lipsett v. *University of Puerto Rico,* 864 F.2d 881 (1st Cir. 1988).

Malin, M. H. "Fathers and Parental Leave Revisited." *Northern Illinois University Law Review,* 1998, *19,* 25.

Mason, M. A., and Goulden, M. "Do Babies Matter? The Effect of Family Formation on the Lifelong Careers of Academic Men and Women." *Academe,* 2002, *88*(6), 21–27.

McCracken, D. M. "Winning the Talent War for Women: Sometimes It Takes a Revolution." *Harvard Business Review,* Nov.–Dec. 2000, pp. 159–164.

Ridgeway, C., and Smith-Lovin, L. "The Gender System and Interaction." *Annual Review of Sociology,* 1999, *25,* 191–216.

Ridgeway, C. L., and Correll, S. "Motherhood as a Status Characteristic." *Journal of Social Issues,* 2004, *60,* 683–700.

Rudman, L. A. "Self Promotion as a Risk Factor for Women: The Cost and Benefit of Counterstereotypical Impressions Management." *Journal of Personality and Social Psychology,* 1998, *74*(3), 629.

Schneider, A. "U. of Oregon Settles Tenure Lawsuit over Maternity Leave." *Chronicle of Higher Education,* July 21, 2000, p. A12.

Schultz, V. "Telling Stories About Women and Work." *Harvard Law Review,* 1990, *103,* 1249.

Sellers, P. "Women, Sex, and Power." *Fortune,* Aug. 5, 1996, p. 42.

Shauman, K. A., and Xie, Y. "Geographic Mobility of Scientists: Sex Differences and Family Constraints." *Demography,* 1996, *33,* 455.

Sweeney v. *Board of Trustees of Keene State College,* 604 F.2d 106 (1st Cir. 1979).

Taylor, S. E. "A Categorization Approach to Stereotyping." In D. L. Hamilton (ed.), *Cognitive Processes in Stereotyping and Intergroup Behavior.* Mahwah, N.J.: Erlbaum, 1981.

Townsend, N. W. *The Package Deal: Marriage, Work, and Fatherhood in Men's Lives.* Philadelphia: Temple University Press, 2002.

Travis, M. A. "Perceived Disabilities, Social Cognition, and 'Innocent Mistakes.'" In J. S. Carroll and J. W. Paynne (eds.), *Cognition and Social Behavior*. Mahwah, N.J.: Erlbaum, 1976.

Valian, V. "The Cognitive Bases of Gender Bias." *Brooklyn Law Review*, 1999, *65*, 1049.

Weinstock v. *Columbia University*, 224 F.3d 33 (2d Cir. 2000).

Williams, J. *Unbending Gender: Why Work and Family Conflict and What to Do About It*. New York: Oxford University Press, 2000.

Williams, J. C., and Segal, N. "Beyond the Maternal Wall: Relief for Family Caregivers Who Are Discriminated Against on the Job." *Harvard Women's Law Journal*, 2003, *26*, 77.

JOAN C. WILLIAMS is professor of law and director of the Program on WorkLife Law, American University, Washington College of Law.

INDEX

Back Issue/Subscription Order Form

Copy or detach and send to:

Jossey-Bass, A Wiley Company, 989 Market Street, San Francisco CA 94103-1741

Call or fax toll-free: Phone 888-378-2537 6:30AM – 3PM PST; Fax 888-481-2665

Back Issues: Please send me the following issues at $29 each
(Important: please include series initials and issue number, such as HE114.)

_____

_____

_____

$ _____   Total for single issues

$ _____   SHIPPING CHARGES: SURFACE   Domestic   Canadian

	Domestic	Canadian
First Item	$5.00	$6.00
Each Add'l Item	$3.00	$1.50

For next-day and second-day delivery rates, call the number listed above.

Subscriptions: Please __start __renew my subscription to *New Directions for Higher Education* for the year 2____at the following rate:

U.S.	__Individual $80	__Institutional $170
Canada	__Individual $80	__Institutional $210
All Others	__Individual $104	__Institutional $244

**For more information about online subscriptions visit
www.interscience.wiley.com**

$ _____   Total single issues and subscriptions (Add appropriate sales tax for your state for single issue orders. No sales tax for U.S. subscriptions. Canadian residents, add GST for subscriptions and single issues.)

__Payment enclosed (U.S. check or money order only)

__VISA __MC __AmEx #_____ Exp. Date _____

Signature _____ Day Phone _____

__ Bill Me (U.S. institutional orders only. Purchase order required.)

Purchase order # _____

Federal Tax ID13559302   **GST 89102 8052**

Name _____

Address _____

Phone _____ E-mail _____

For more information about Jossey-Bass, visit our Web site at **www.josseybass.com**

NEW DIRECTIONS FOR HIGHER EDUCATION IS NOW AVAILABLE ONLINE AT WILEY INTERSCIENCE

What is Wiley InterScience?

Wiley InterScience is the dynamic online content service from John Wiley & Sons delivering the full text of over 300 leading scientific, technical, medical, and professional journals, plus major reference works, the acclaimed *Current Protocols* laboratory manuals, and even the full text of select Wiley print books online.

What are some special features of Wiley InterScience?

Wiley InterScience Alerts is a service that delivers table of contents via e-mail for any journal available on Wiley InterScience as soon as a new issue is published online.

Early View is Wiley's exclusive service presenting individual articles online as soon as they are ready, even before the release of the compiled print issue. These articles are complete, peer-reviewed, and citable.

CrossRef is the innovative multi-publisher reference linking system enabling readers to move seamlessly from a reference in a journal article to the cited publication, typically located on a different server and published by a different publisher.

How can I access Wiley InterScience?

Visit http://www.interscience.wiley.com

Guest Users can browse Wiley InterScience for unrestricted access to journal Tables of Contents and Article Abstracts, or use the powerful search engine.

Registered Users are provided with a *Personal Home Page* to store and manage customized alerts, searches, and links to favorite journals and articles. Additionally, Registered Users can view free Online Sample Issues and preview selected material from major reference works.

Licensed Customers are entitled to access full-text journal articles in PDF, with select journals also offering full-text HTML.

How do I become an Authorized User?

Authorized Users are individuals authorized by a paying Customer to have access to the journals in Wiley InterScience. For example, a university that subscribes to Wiley journals is considered to be the Customer. Faculty, staff and students authorized by the university to have access to those journals in Wiley InterScience are Authorized Users. Users should contact their Library for information on which Wiley journals they have access to in Wiley InterScience.

ASK YOUR INSTITUTION ABOUT WILEY INTERSCIENCE TODAY!